Women Who Made Bible History

Women Who Made Bible History

Messages and Character Sketches
Dealing with Familiar Bible Women

by

HAROLD JOHN OCKENGA

Pastor, Park Street Church, Boston
President, Fuller Theological Seminary

ZONDERVAN PUBLISHING HOUSE
GRAND RAPIDS   MICHIGAN

TABLE OF CONTENTS

Women Who Made Bible History

1

Eve

THE MOTHER OF ALL LIVING

*And Adam called his wife's name Eve; because she was
the mother of all living* (Gen. 3:20).

Eve was called by Adam "the mother of all living." In the
first three chapters of Genesis we find all the principles which
are later expounded in Scripture and applicable unto our lives,
including creation, temptation and sin, and redemption. The
center of interest in this narrative is Eve.

The steps in the creation process were gradual. Five
times the Bible says, "And God saw that it was good." The
last step in the creation process was when "the Lord God
formed man of the dust of the ground, and breathed into his
nostrils the breath of life; and man became a living soul"
(Gen. 2:7). Then we read, "The Lord God planted a garden
eastward in Eden; and there he put the man whom he had
formed." This environment for man was absolutely perfect.
What a glorious garden it was! In it was everything that was
good: every kind of flower which was beautiful to the eye,
every tree upon which man loves to look, every shrub to break
the abruptness of contrast between the trees and flowers,
every herb, every vine and every moss, every lichen which
would contribute to the beauty of the place. Trees, shrubs
and plants which we would travel far to see were there in
great profusion and yet in order and in loveliness. This was a
garden, not a jungle. There was no thorn, no briar or thistle
or weed. There was only profuse beauty, perfumed fragrance,
panorama of color and valuable plants.

In this garden there was no death. All animals, from the least to the greatest, were there, named by the first man and manifesting the beauty of their strength and nature, but they were not beasts of prey. They all lived together in harmony. They were vegetarian and to them was given such a range of food that they never desired the flesh of another animal. Hence, in that garden was no pain, no disease, no hurt and no sorrow. Instead, there was nothing but happiness, pleasure and delight for all creatures living in pristine harmony and glory. There was not even a rain cloud in the sky, for the Lord did not cause it to rain upon the earth but watered it by means of a mist that came up from the earth. The garden of Eden was all that the wisdom of an infinite God could make it in perfection. Every lover of nature who delights in a scene of tranquility in the hills or the lakes, whose soul is enraptured with the beauty of an ancient oak or fir, who loves the micaflaked rocks of the mountains, experiences a throwback to what the first man and woman must have experienced in the garden of Eden.

The State of Woman as Created

The garden in which God placed man and woman was possible only after the six stages of creation which are described in the first chapter of Genesis. The Bible accurately describes the wonders of those six creative days and in this we read nothing which is contrary to the discoveries of science. The first day speaks of God's creating the heavens and the earth. Some think that the Bible then immediately describes a judgment upon the earth as it originally was created in perfection, for the second verse of Genesis speaks of the earth being without form and void. Later, Isaiah said, using these very words, that God did not create the world without form or void (Isa. 45:18), so some think that this was a time in which Satan was judged and the world became a great void. Following this came the six creative days or stages of remodeling of the earth. Whether one accepts this theory or not, the six stages of the process of creation are clearly delineated. If, in that original judgment, mountains were heaved up, vast forests were covered, deposits of oil were laid in the earth, fossils were caught in the liquid rock, then the six creative days would be that of remodeling the earth rather than original stages of creation. Possibly we will never know what method God used in His bringing to pass the earth as we now know it.

The first stage describes the bringing forth the light of the sun which had already been created but which was shrouded in the mists of darkness. The second stage was that of creating the airy and gaseous heavens beyond which is darkness and without which there would be no diffusion of light and hence life upon the earth.

In the third period the Lord brought forth the land out of the waters and caused the land to bring forth grass, herbs, fruit trees and plant life, each seed yielding after its kind. On the fourth creative day God made the lights of the firmament to appear and set them as signs and for seasons, and days and years, to rule over the changes of the earth. In the fifth stage, the Lord exercised His power of creation and brought forth the living things in the waters, and also the fowl of the heaven. In the sixth stage, God caused the earth to bring forth all forms of animals after their own kind so that the earth was filled with animals and this also was pronounced good.

The final stage of creation was that of making man. It is interesting that this appearance of man occurs in the same stage or era as that in which God caused the earth to bring forth the living creatures, the beasts of the field, but that God made man in His own image, thus differentiating him from all of the beasts of the field.

Three major declarations are made in this first text concerning the creation of man. First, he was made in the image of God. This image is spiritual, moral and intellectual. Spiritually, man is of one kind with God and possesses a derived immortality. Intellectually, he is capable of thinking God's thoughts after Him. Morally, he can make the decisions which will reveal his kinship to deity. The second great declaration about man is that he was to have dominion over all of the creation. This fact is restated several times in the Scripture and should remove all provincialism as to man's ability to master scientifically the world in which he lives. The third fact declared about man is that God created him male and female. It is on this that Jesus bases His teaching concerning monogamous marriage, saying, "From the beginning of the creation God made them male and female. For this cause shall a man leave his father and mother, and cleave to his wife; and they twain shall be one flesh" (Matt. 19:5).

Generically speaking, man was the highest in God's series of creation. The word "create" is used three times in the first chapter of Genesis. The first time is when it says, "In the beginning God created the heaven and the earth" (vs. 1). The second time is when God created life, and it says, "And God created . . . every living creature that moveth" (vs. 21). The third is when God created man and it says, "So God created man in his own image" (vs. 27). At these three points the materialistic evolutionists are forever hindered because they cannot produce any theory which accounts for the beginning of the world, or the beginning of man. As for the world, either it must have eternally existed or else it must have been created. There is no middle ground. The theist believes that God created it. As for life, there has never been any demonstration of a spontaneous origin of life or even an artificial creation of life on the part of man. Life must have had a beginning somewhere. As for man himself, although many theories may be advanced as to primitive man, or preadamic man, yet the Bible clearly says that God created man and at some point, regardless of whether God used dust of the ground or whether He used an animal whom He had already created, He bridged the gap between by breathing into man the breath of life and making Him in His own image.

Between the various stages of creation there is large room for theories of development. We have no means of knowing how long the creative days were which are spoken of in the first chapter of the book of Genesis. They may have been long eras of time and it may have been the good pleasure of God to develop the species by gradual processes as well as by sudden act. At the end of this great process before what the Bible describes as God's sabbath rest, the final act of deity was the creation of woman. She was not only the last but she was the best. She was absolutely perfect. One woman may resemble the Venus de Milo, another may have a mind of keenest power, another may have a rare spirit, but with any human being today there is some limitation. But if we could combine the best of body, mind and spirit into one, we would have some idea of the first woman whom God created.

The story of the creation of woman in Genesis 2:18-24 is suggestive as to the position which she should have as a help-mate for man. Although man had a perfect place in which to live, every imaginable kind of beast and bird creature with which to work or play, he was nevertheless alone. There was a wide gulf which separated him from every creature of the world. He recognized that he was of a different quality of being. Man for awhile may be satisfied with horses and dogs and birds, but he cannot be permanently so. God said, "It is not good that the man should be alone; I will make him an help meet for him" (Gen. 2:18).

Ancient commentators were accustomed to refer to the method which God used in creating woman in order to show her position in relationship to man. They said, "God did not make woman from man's head, as Hera is supposed to have sprung full-grown from the head of Job, lest man worship her. He did not take woman from man's feet lest man use her as a slave. God took woman from one of his ribs near his heart in order that he might love her and recognize her as equal, protecting her with the power of his arm."

The original relationship between man and woman was that of monogamous marriage. In response to the disciples' question about divorce, the Lord Jesus said, "Have ye not read, that he which made them at the beginning made them male and female, and said, For this cause shall a man leave father and mother, and shall cleave to his wife: and they twain shall be one flesh? Wherefore they are no more twain, but one flesh. What therefore God hath joined together, let not man put asunder." With the exception of the last clause of this statement, this question is taken from the book of Genesis. Any departure in history from this high standard is according to Christ permitted only because of the hardness of men's hearts, but in the beginning it was not so, for God intended man and woman to live together in a monogamous relationship of marriage. It has been shown that several inferences can be drawn from Christ's comment. First, the twofold purpose of marriage is mutual companionship and happiness and the propagation of the race. The fact of the marriage of one man and one woman, contrary to all other social theories, was the original relationship and the plan of God. Second, there was no provision made for the dissolution of marriage. Third, there was no provision made for sex relationship between men and women outside of marriage. Fourth, human marriage was to be fruitful and a means to replenish the earth. Fifth, there was no provision made for a trial marriage or for a series of marriages: a marriage was to be unto death.

The first marriage between man and woman must have been an extremely happy one. Theirs were scenes of fellowship and love as they lived together in the garden and walked with God in the cool of the day. Theirs was unclotted bliss, perfect understanding and an endless love. Theirs was the ideal marriage, the ideal love and the ideal happiness. Moreover, they were blessed by the presence of God who walked with them in the cool of the day. God made man for fellowship and enjoyment and He revealed His affection to man in this garden fellowship. To walk with God is the highest privilege which is given to man upon earth. Adam and Eve enjoyed undimmed fellowship with their Creator.

In the midst of this fellowship, the Lord established a commandment, or a probation for the first man and woman. He said, "Of every tree of the garden thou mayest freely eat: but of the tree of the knowledge of good and evil, thou shalt not eat of it: for in the day that thou eatest thereof thou shalt surely die" (Gen. 2:16,17). We also read of the tree of life which was in the midst of the garden, but of no command that man should not eat of it. It is possible that this was permitted to see whether man would eat first of the tree of life which would confirm him in his likeness to God or whether he would first eat of the tree of the knowledge of good and evil and thus fall from his position of primitive creation.

This commandment of God is known as the covenant of works. It is the requirement that man shall live by doing. Works were later enlarged in the ten commandments and again enlarged in the Sermon on the Mount. Its requirement is that of perfect obedience. In the day that man violates the commandment of God, he will surely die. Perfect obedience is necessary to possess eternal life, hence it excludes all men from salvation by works, for no man from Adam until now has lived in perfect obedience to the commandments of God with the exception of the Lord Jesus Christ. When the lawyer asked Jesus, "What good thing shall I do, that I may have eternal life?" He said, "Keep the commandments" (Matt. 19:16,17). If a man could fulfill all God's commandments, he could live by them. But it was during this period of probation that the temptation came and man fell.

The Woman as Temptress

The fact that Eve became a temptress assumes that she had fallen. In order to be the instrument of evil, Eve first had to subject herself to evil. Hence, we turn our attention to the temptation of the woman by the serpent. The Scripture truly says that the devil assumed the form of a serpent. In this we have a suggestion of what must have happened in the pre-earthly ages when Satan fell from his high position as Lucifer, the angel of the morning, and began his activity of contending against God in every form in which he could (Isa. 14:12-17).

The methods used by Satan in tempting Eve are the methods which he uses in his activities in the world today. His temptation of the woman is almost identical with his temptation of the Lord Jesus. He appealed to them both through the lust of the eye, the love of the world and the pride of life. First, Satan questioned the authority of the Word of God. He said, "Hath God said?" He suggested that the commandment which they had received was not from God at all. After the woman reiterated the commandment because she knew it well, he then questioned the truth of what God had said, "Ye shall not surely die." Finally, he questioned the justice in the commandment and the motive of God in giving the commandment. He said, "For God doth know that in the day ye eat thereof, then your eyes shall be opened, and ye shall be as gods, knowing good and evil." The study of the temptation of the first woman, or of Job, or of Jesus Christ reveals the same suggestion. Satan thought that when Christ saw the kingdoms of the world He would fall down and worship him, or that when He heard a misquotation of the Word of God, He would in presumption act upon it, or that He could be enticed and use His power for His own purposes. These methods were successful in seducing the woman. The Bible says, "When the woman saw that the tree was good for food, and that it was pleasant to the eyes, and a tree to be desired to make one wise, she took of the fruit thereof, and did eat." Briefly, she considered it, she desired it and she partook of it. Once the woman had sinned, Satan was now able to do his work through her as the temptress. The Bible does not tell us of Satan's appearance to or conversation with the man. He now committed his cause to the woman who became the temptress.

A description of the fall of Adam is very simple. The Bible says, "The woman . . . gave also unto her husband with her; and he did eat." Man rationally, intentionally and voluntarily entered into sin. Probably Adam resisted this in the beginning, but the influence of Eve wore him down, as the wife of Potiphar prevailed upon him, as the daughter of Timnath prevailed upon Samson and as has happened so often in human history. Adam weighed the consequences well. He knew what it meant. He remembered the time when he was alone and he anticipated a time when the woman would be judged and he would be left alone again, so he made his choice deliberately. He chose the presence of the woman whom he loved, with sin, rather than holiness without her. Thus, both man and woman sinned, and as the mother and father of all living, they communicated to all men the guilt of this sin and the propensity to further sin.

That there was guilt in the action of Eve and of Adam is evident from the fact that their eyes were opened and they knew that they were naked. Their innocence was gone. The half-truth which Satan told was fulfilled. They now were as God. They knew the difference between right and wrong, but they also carried with them the terrible sense of guilt because they had transgressed the commandment of God. When the voice of God sought Adam out in the cool of the day, saying, "Where art thou?" Adam responded, "I heard thy voice in the garden, and I was afraid, because I was naked; and I hid myself."

The subsequent inquisition for guilt made by God placed the primary responsibility upon the devil and the secondary responsibility upon man and woman and punishments were fitted to each. Enmity was to exist between the serpent and the seed of the woman and a physical change was to come upon the serpent itself. The punishment of the woman was that in sorrow she should bring forth children. The punishment of Adam was that the ground was to be cursed for his sake and in sorrow he should eat of it all the days of his life.

Eve as the Means of Victory Over Temptation

In the midst of the curse upon woman, however, there came a promise. God said to the serpent, "I will put enmity . . . between thy seed and her seed; it shall bruise thy head, and thou shalt bruise his heel." This prophecy begins a chain of references in the Bible which lead directly to the coming of Christ and His redemptive work on Calvary. Eve understood this and she believed the promise which is later enlarged for her descendants until the time of Christ. In Christ's death upon the cross He was bruised, but there He bruised the head of Satan and won a final victory. When Christ went to Calvary, He said, "Now shall the prince of this world be cast out" (John

12:31). Satan's power was broken at Calvary. Christ is the Lamb of God that taketh away the sin of the world.

The belief of this promise by Eve is shown in the naming of her firstborn son (Gen. 4:1). The original Hebrew text says, "Eve conceived and bare Cain and said, I have gotten a man, the Lord." Eve thought that the promise of the Messiah, or Saviour, who was to be born of woman and to be God was fulfilled in her firstborn son, Cain. The promise was not to be fulfilled until Mary heard the words of the angel Gabriel who said, "That holy thing which shall be born of thee shall be called the Son of God" (Luke 1:35). Yet this belief had lighted the hopes of holy women and holy men throughout the ages.

When God finished conversing with man, we read, "The Lord God made coats of skins, and clothed them." These were a divinely intended type of Christ who was made unto us righteousness, which righteousness is the garment by which sinners are clothed and made fit for the presence of God. As those animals were a substitute for Adam and Eve, so Christ is the substitute for us. God overlooked the sins which were past in the light of the sacrifice which was to come (Rom. 3:24-26).

2

Sarah

THE MOTHER OF A NATION

> *And I will bless her, and give thee a son also of her: yea,
> I will bless her and she shall be a mother of nations;
> kings of people shall be of her* (Gen. 17:16).

Sarah in Scripture is called the mother of the "families of
the earth." The knowledge we have of Sarah is derived from
the knowledge we have of Abraham. For this she is commended by Peter (I Peter 3:6). The only record we have of
Sarah is that of a devoted wife throughout her entire life. She
is introduced to us as the wife of Abraham and as such she
died. As the wife of her husband, she fulfilled all demands of
God's precepts. Great emphasis has been placed upon the fact
that Abraham obeyed God and it was counted unto him for
righteousness. He obeyed God when he left Ur of the Chaldees at the command of God in order to go into a land which
he knew not. Let us not forget that Sarah also left Ur of Chaldees along with Abraham with just as great a venture of faith
as he faced. In fact, it is much harder on a woman to leave
her native land and kindred and friends than it is for a man.

Even the lineage of Sarah is traced through her husband
rather than through herself. She is called "the daughter of
Abraham's father but not of his mother." The common Jewish
tradition accepted by Jerome and Josephus is that Sarah was
the daughter of Haran, the brother of Abraham, who died in
Ur of Chaldees and hence, she was Abraham's own niece.
Thus he could refer to her as his sister as he did on several
occasions to save them both from death. Sarah shared Abra-

19

ham's wanderings, his defections due to his weakness of faith, and his great triumphs which caused him to be called the father of the faithful and "the friend of God," until at the advanced age of 127 years she died and was buried in the cave of Machpelah, the only piece of ground which Abraham owned in the promised land.

The name Sarai which belonged to Abraham's wife before their names were changed means "my princess." This suggests two beautiful things: First, the fact that Sarah was a woman of high social standing in the country from which she came; and second, that she stood in a very endearing relationship to her husband Abraham. If one considers that Ur of Chaldees was the center of philosophy, astronomy and culture of that ancient day, we realize what Sarah left to travel with Abraham. The Scripture refers to her as being "fair" and "very fair" and "lovely to look upon." The Dead Sea Scrolls at the Hebrew University on Mount Scopus refer to Sarah in the book of Genesis as "how fair indeed are her eyes and how pleasing her nose and all the radiance of her face . . . and how lovely all her whiteness . . . her arms how goodly to look upon, and her hands how perfect." Wherever Sarah journeyed, the admiring eyes of people were upon her and she was coveted for the harems of the rulers of those lands.

Her name was changed from Sarai to Sarah at the same time that Abraham's name was changed from Abram to Abraham. The adding of the syllable, or consonant, to the names of these two persons represented Jehovah and it was a symbol of the establishment of the covenant between God and Abraham's house. The sign of that covenant was circumcision. The essence of it was that God had chosen Abraham and his seed to be the recipients of the Messianic promise in recognition of which he would give to Abraham the land of Canaan and would be Abraham's God. To Sarah God promised that He would give a son and that she should be the mother of nations. Not only is Abraham listed in the roster of the heroes of the faith in Hebrews 11, but Sarah is also listed. There we read, "Through faith also Sara herself received strength to conceive seed, and was delivered of a child when she was past age, because she judged him faithful who had promised." She also was one who "through faith . . . obtained promises" and "of whom the world was not worthy."

Sarah had her shortcomings and at times was guilty of unbelief, but the great characteristic of her life is faith. In her we see a beautiful, cultured princess, who because of faith in the promise of God, underwent great sacrifices. Her experience illustrates the various kinds of relationship which a soul can have to God, all of which may be subsumed under the word "laughter" which is the meaning of "Isaac," the name she gave to her son.

The Laugh of Unbelief

Abraham and Sarah both laughed at the promise of God and in both cases their laugh was that of unbelief. When we understand the entire circumstances, we will not condemn them for their act of laughing at God's promise. One of the means used by God in revealing His will unto men in the early stage of divine revelation was by means of a theophany, or His appearance in human form. He appeared to and conversed with men. This is the kind of communion which Adam had with God. It is the kind of communion enjoyed by Enoch when it said Enoch "walked with God." (Gen. 5:24). The Lord on several occasions appeared unto Abraham and also to Sarah, his wife. When God first appeared unto Abraham on this matter, commanding Abraham to change Sarah's name, promising to Abraham a son by Sarah, and prophesying that Sarah would become a mother of nations, Abraham fell upon his face and laughed (Gen. 17:17). The incongruity of a woman nearly ninety years of age bearing a child after the couple had waited for so many years for the promise to be fulfilled in vain, made Abraham laugh. In response, he said, "O that Ishmael might live before thee!" But the Lord reiterated His promise and commanded Abraham to call the child Isaac, or "laughter," to remind him of this unbelief.

At some time later the Lord appeared again unto Abraham as he sat in the door of his tent. Apparently Abraham recognized Him for he said, "My Lord, if now I have found favour in thy sight, pass not away, I pray thee, from thy servant." Abraham insisted on extending hospitality. When the New Testament says that some have entertained angels unawares, it refers to this among other instances. Though Abraham.knew that he was entertaining a theophany of God and two angels, Sarah entertained them unawares. Sarah herself even cooked the meal which was set before these messengers of God. It consisted of tender calf, butter, milk and freshly made bread and it was given in a spirit of gladness.

When the meal was over, the spokesman said, "Where is Sarah thy wife?" Abraham replied, "Behold, in the tent." Then said the angel of the Lord, "I will certainly return unto thee according to the time of life; and, lo, Sarah thy wife shall have a son." Sarah had waited and longed so long for a child that now the incongruity of the thing struck her because of her age. She had even been willing that Abraham should have a son through Hagar, which expedient had brought forth Ishmael. For her now to have a child would be the result of a definite creative act of God. When Sarah heard these words pronounced to Abraham, she laughed within her heart, thinking that this was absolutely impossible (Gen. 19:12). Hers was a laugh of irony, of unbelief, of doubt that such a promise should be reiterated when now it was impossible. This laughter in Sarah was not that of an unbeliever. It was that of a believer who did not trust a particular divine promise. Her laughter was not that of mockery but it was that one single act of unbelief in the life of a believing person. It was spontaneous unbelief at the incongruity of the thing that a woman nearly 90 years old should have a son. She was considering the whole situation from the purely human side and not from the divine side.

The laughter of Sarah was quite unlike the laughter of men who mock God today. Men who laugh at God with the mockery of unbelief, who ridicule and hate the promises, who repudiate the Gospel, have their laughter originate in basic wickedness and antipathy to God in the degenerate human heart. This laughter is akin to the mockery made of Christ when on the cross men said unto Him, "If thou be the Son of God, come down from the cross." Modern mockery is centered in the intellectualism of our day which would confine God to natural law and laughs at any promise that God can intervene in the natural course of events so as to perform a miracle, to fulfill prophecy or to answer prayer. For this reason they brand passages in the book of Daniel, of Isaiah and Amos as written after the events. For this reason they laugh at the idea of a virgin birth. For this reason they repudiate the Biblical teaching of a physical resurrection and for this reason they mock the Biblical teaching concerning the second coming of Christ in glory.

Such laughter at God and the promises of God leads one to inevitable sorrow and trouble. The first outcome is sin, for unbelief blasts one's faith in the abiding values of life and brings about an utter disregard of ethical standards. Once God is reasoned away, or laughed away, all moral standards which depend upon the belief in God will be laughed away. This might be illustrated from the way Communism, which is founded upon atheism, destroys all moral and human values. Once you laugh at God in unbelief you will begin to live as if there were no God.

THE LAUGH OF FAITH

The evidence of Scripture is that the lives of Abraham and Sarah were not marked by permanent unbelief but rather by faith. For this reason they are given their position in the roster of the heroes of the faith. Of Sarah it is said, "Through faith also Sarah herself received strength to conceive seed . . . when she was past age" (Heb. 11:11). Thus, Sarah exercised faith which is pleasing to God. It is interesting that when Sarah laughed in her heart, God knew that she had laughed, for the Lord said unto Abraham, "Wherefore did Sarah laugh, saying, Shall I of a surety bear a child, which am old? Is any thing too hard for the Lord?" Then He reiterated the promise that He would now give unto Abraham and Sarah a son.

Very sobering is the thought here emphasized, that **God** knows the unspoken thoughts of our hearts. John tells us that there is no use in our praying for spiritual objects if we regard iniquity within our hearts, for the Lord will not hear us. There is no use pretending that we believe the promises if we laugh at them secretly within our hearts. All such actions are known to God. Christ was able to tell men their thoughts before they ever expressed them and the Lord reads the unspoken attitudes of our hearts. When Sarah heard this, she denied that she had laughed, saying, "I laughed not." Truly, she had not laughed openly, she had not even so much as smiled, but in her heart, deep down, she had laughed at the incongruity of a woman of her age having a child. Christ taught that men were guilty of adultery if they looked upon a woman to lust after her in their hearts and that they are guilty of murder if they even are angry with their brothers in their hearts. Thus the Lord drives our religion deep down into the heart and He rebuked Sarah because she laughed secretly. Surely, when the Lord reiterated His promise to Sarah and Abraham, they should have believed and not have needed the third statement of the divine promise. It seems that this very rebuke of the Lord caused a change in Sarah from unbelief to faith so that she thereafter was able to act upon the promise. It was at this time that the physical vigor of Sarah and Abraham was divinely renewed so that Sarah again became a great beauty and Abraham continued in the vigor of manhood for the rest of his life. This continuance of strength revealed that Sarah and Abraham continued in faith in accordance with the divine promise, for the New Testament says, "She judged [the Lord] faithful who had promised" (Heb. 11:11).

When the Lord spoke to Abraham, He said, "Is any thing too hard for the Lord?" (Gen. 18:14.) This promise of what the Lord was able to perform for this aged couple reminds us of the promise and of the wonderful creative act of God in bringing the Lord Jesus into the world through a virgin birth. When the angel Gabriel made the annunciation unto Mary that the child which should be born of her should be called the Son of God, she asked, "How shall this be?" Then Gabriel replied, "With God nothing shall be impossible" (Luke 1:37). It was not a stretch of imagination after such a visitation of God and the special reiterated promise that Abraham and Sarah did believe that Isaac was to become the Messiah as is intimated by Abraham's believing that God could raise him from the dead if he sacrificed him on Mount Moriah.

It is this principle that nothing is impossible with God that made the men of faith throughout the ages do wonderful things. The generation of Noah mocked his preaching, ridiculed his building of the ark, and rejected his message because there had never been a flood. In fact, it is probable there never had been any rain. But Noah believed God and built an ark to the saving of his house.

Moses stood before Pharaoh with faith in the God of the burning bush and demanded the release of the Israelites. Pharaoh laughed and said, "Who is the Lord, that I should obey his voice to let Israel go?" But in response to Moses' faith in the God of the impossible, two million people were delivered from Egypt and the armies of Egypt were overcome in the Red Sea.

When David visited the armies of Israel which were being defied by Goliath, the champion of the Philistines, he said, "Who is this . . . that he should defy the armies of the living God? . . . Thy servant will go and fight with this Philistine" (I Sam. 17). In the name of the Lord God of Hosts, David went forth with his staff and with a slingshot to meet Goliath, the man of war, and overcame him. He believed that nothing was impossible with God. The Scripture says of the heroes of the faith that they "through faith subdued kingdoms, wrought righteousness, obtained promises, stopped the mouths of lions, quenched the violence of fire, escaped the edge of the sword, out of weakness were made strong, waxed valiant in fight, turned to flight the armies of the aliens. Women received their dead raised to life again: and others were tortured, not accepting deliverance; that they might obtain a better resurrection . . . of whom the world was not worthy" (Heb. 11:33-35, 38).

Thus it is that the world laughs at faith but faith laughs at the world. Instead of being defeated by the mockery and ridicule of the world, men of faith are able to laugh at all obstacles and to overcome them through the God of the impossible.

The Laughter of Joy

The Scripture says the Lord did as He said unto Sarah. The day came when her son was born, when the joy of the fulfilled promise belonged unto Sarah. Bear in mind that on four occasions God had said unto Abraham and Sarah that He would give them a son through whom the nations of the world should be blessed. He had promised that the seed of Abraham should be as innumerable as the stars in the heavens and as the sands of the seashore for multitude. Just as their expectancy had led them to an act of unbelief in substituting Hagar as a mother of the promised seed, so now their expectation led them to an expression of joy when it was fulfilled. They had waited long and had prayed much for this promise to be fulfilled. Now, by a supernatural act of God, it came to pass.

Sarah named her son "Isaac" which means laughter, because she said, "God hath made me to laugh, so that all that hear will laugh with me" (Gen. 21:6). Believing him to be the progenitor of the Messiah, if not the Messiah Himself, her laugh was the laugh of salvation, it was the laugh of the joy of knowing that one's sins are forgiven through the man whom God has sent. Through this son of Sarah all the nations of the earth were to be blessed, through the tidings of salvation. How wonderfully all has been fulfilled in the descendant of Isaac, namely, the Lord Jesus Christ. Wherever the name of Jesus has gone as Saviour, there has been joy unspeakable and full of of glory, joy of sins forgiven, joy of victory, joy of possessing a heavenly promise. All this Sarah and Abraham felt when Isaac was born.

This laughter of joy was the laughter of trusting God's promise. After this, Abraham was put to test by the command to sacrifice his son Isaac on Mount Moriah. Men have honored Abraham for his obedience to this command of God but did

Sarah have no suffering, no expression of faith when she faced the command? Are we to believe that Sarah did not know what Abraham intended when he left with Isaac, the servants, the wood, the knife and the fire? The intimate relationship of Abraham and Sarah would have prevented his hiding his purpose from her. Though it may not have been stated, nevertheless Sarah could tell by the look in his eye, by the suffering written upon his brow, by the circumstances of his leaving what his purpose was. What agony of soul she must have passed through while Abraham and Isaac were gone on that trip to Mount Moriah! What consecration it took for her not to stand in the way of her husband's purpose! If Abraham believed that God could raise Isaac from the dead and restore him unto him, Sarah must also have believed this. Hence, we have in Isaac not only a type of the death and resurrection of our Lord Jesus Christ but also a type of true faith on the part of these two parents who resigned themselves to the necessary death of their divinely sent son for the salvation of themselves and the world.

An old Jewish legend stated by Josephus is that when Abraham and Isaac returned from Mount Moriah, they found Sarah dying of a broken heart. The terrible ordeal had been too much for her. Shortly after this, Abraham laid her away in the cave of Machpelah where he himself was later to be buried. The return of Isaac with his father was a vindication of the divine purposes and promises in relation to Isaac. Sarah and Abraham had the joy of trusting these promises.

Theirs was also the joy of salvation through the fulfillment of the promise of Christ, for what Isaac presented to them the Lord Jesus Christ represents to us. Where Christ is not known, there is no laughter, there is no joy, there is no peace, but wherever He is known, the laughter of joy follows. Truly every soul who trusts in Christ may laugh, rejoice and sing for joy. Thus, as Abraham is the father of the faithful, Sarah is the mother of spiritual nations.

3

Rachel

THE WOMAN WHO COMMANDED A MAN'S LOVE

> And Jacob served seven years for Rachel and they seemed
> unto him but a few days, for the love he had to her
> (Gen. 29:20).

There is no other case recorded in the Bible of such abiding love as that which Jacob had for Rachel. This, in fact, is the best type of Christ's love for the church that is given to us. He loved her from the very beginning; he suffered for her; and he loved her to the end in spite of the blemishes in her character.

There is another love recorded in secular history somewhat similar to the love of Jacob for Rachel, which stimulated the man who possessed it to a marvelous achievement. I speak of Dante's love for Beatrice Portinari. This love inspired his life and enlarged his soul to the extent that he devoted his genius to her eulogy. Dante was born in the year 1265 and met Beatrice when he was only nine years old, but he at once conceived the highest and most enduring love for her. During the next nine years he met her only on one other occasion, during which she bestowed on him a celestial smile of recognition. Three years later, at the age of twenty-four, she died, and Dante determined to write of her such as was never written of any woman. Dante was a member of what is called the Guelf Party, composed of the common people in Florence and allied with Roman Catholicism. The opposing party was called the Ghebelline Party and was composed of the imperial, or

29

state, unit. During Dante's life there was a constant struggle between the two, and while he was absent from Florence at one time his enemies secured his banishment. Thereafter he wandered throughout the cities of Italy engaged in literary work until he died at the age of fifty-six at Ravenna. Dante had married a daughter of one of the leaders of the Guelf Party and was the father of eight children but never during his life did he lose his idealistic love for Beatrice. Hence it was to her that he raised the monument of his love. No writer since the rise of the Romantic School of literature, when love became the chief theme of poetry, has so reverently worshiped and so happily embodied the highest ideals of womanhood as Dante. Here love was unrequited and in sorrow, anguish, and tears its possessor was driven to despair. It was the image of this gentle vision that warmed and purified his soul and inspired his deeds until he became the "voice of ten silent centuries." She became a comforting, guiding spirit and illumined with intense joy the poet's heart, hitherto one of the saddest in all Christendom.

Thus it was that Dante — hereafter to be known to the world as the noblest of all lovers, when Dante the statesman, the philosopher, the Guelphic leader shall be forgotten — vowed that "if it would please Him by whom all things live, he would say of her that which had never been said of any lady." She became his muse. It was a message from her which led him down through the gates of Despair, across the Limbo that trembled with the sighs of hopeless longing, past Minos, judge of Hades, into the flaming City of Dis, garrisoned and guarded by demons and furies, past the Hell of Violence, where murderers and tyrants are forever steeped in the boiling blood waves of the Plegethon; through the increasing horrors of Circles, Evil-pits, and Bealts of Treachery; then up the toilsome steps of Purgatory, until at last appeared, drawn in the bosom of a cloud of flowers, thrown by angel hands, the radiant form of Beatrice clad in white, green, and red emblems of faith, hope, and charity. Thus this love for a young woman whom he had seen only twice in his life caused Dante to be remembered throughout the ages.

Likewise, the one ennobling influence in the life of Jacob was his love for Rachel. Through Rachel, God brought retribution to Jacob for his many sins in order to purify his soul. The beginning of this was the deception wrought on Jacob by Laban, the father of Rachel, when, after Jacob had served seven years for her, he was given the veiled Leah in the night and learned that he must serve a second seven years for the object of his love. There Jacob must have seen the hand of God requiting him for the deception he had wrought over the eyes of his old father in taking Esau's blessing. The next time his love for Rachel led him to recognize the hand of God was when he was returning frob Padan-aram and met a messenger who said that Esau was coming to meet him with four hundred armed men. Jacob knew that his own life and the lives of his entire company were hanging by a thread. The prayer he prayed unto God by Peniel before he wrestled with the angel reveals to us what was uppermost in Jacob's mind. He said, "Deliver me, I pray Thee from the hand of Esau: for I fear him, lest he will come and smite me, and the mother with the children." It was the thought of Rachel and Rachel's child Joseph and the one who was yet to be born that drove Jacob to his knees as he wrestled with the angel of God. Finally, the Lord dealt with Jacob through the death of Rachel and the loss of her children, both Joseph and Benjamin, one of whom was sold into Egypt and the other of whom was compelled to go thence because of the famine, so that Jacob said to his other sons, "My son shall not go down with you for his brother is dead and he is left alone. If mischief befall him by the way in which he goes, then shall ye bring down my gray hairs with sorrow to the grave" (Gen. 42:38). The loss of Benjamin, the last of his family by Rachel, would have been the final straw in Jacob's sorrow. Thus we see that by his great love which Jacob bore to Rachel, God chastened and purified his soul. Woman has been the divine instrument in the salvation of man in all ages; for the love he bears her he is lifted to nobility, to purity, and to sacrificial living. A woman who can command his love can command the best of which he is capable.

I. The Incident That Led to Their Meeting

Providence has a place in the bringing of two streams of life together. This must be recognized not only with Jacob and Rachel but in the uniting of any young man and young woman in love. Marriage was instituted of God so that one life may supplement another. Rebecca was exactly the opposite of Isaac, but her dynamic nature was just what passive Isaac needed. Just so, Rachel took her position in relation to Jacob. He needed a mooring for his emotions. He needed an anchor for his wandering soul, and he found that abiding place in Rachel. Never do I stand before a couple presenting themselves for marriage without thinking of the long line of history each represents and how they will be merged as two great rivers are merged, thus strengthening one another and empowering one another. They come together to purify and to bless. Thus it was meant to be. Morever, Providence had a hand in the ordering of events so that these two streams of life should come together. Sometimes observers of a wedding or of a romance cannot see what a man sees in the woman or the woman sees in the man, but there is a purpose in it. The parents of Samson could not understand why he passed by all the beautiful daughters of the Israelites and became enamored with the Philistine woman who dwelt at Timnath and asked for her for his wife, but the Scripture says that God sought an occasion against the Philistines (Judg. 14:4). The purpose was that Samson through this incident should be established as judge over the Israelites, whom he thereafter ruled for twenty years. Every married person may trace the events that led to his union with another person. Sometimes it is a chance meeting in a library or on a street-car or in a church or at a party, an incident that happened only because some other less important incident occurred before, and the whole course of life was

changed. Thus we affirm that Providence has a part in bringing people together in marriage.

A second thing that contributed to Jacob's going to Haran
was his early waywardness. This had its roots in his mother's
partiality. From the beginning it seemed that Rebecca favored
Jacob, whereas Isaac loved Esau, and there was a house divided against itself (Gen. 25:28). Why was Rebecca so partial
to Jacob? We know that Isaac loved Esau because he ate of
his son's venison. Perhaps Rebecca's prejudice was due to the
promise the Lord made to her before the birth of her son,
which said, "The elder shall serve the younger." Paul later
quotes this promise, saying, "That the purpose of God according to election might stand" (Rom. 9:11). From the divine
side, Jacob was elected, but from the human side Rebecca
pushed him by partiality. Undoubtedly this mother taught her
son the value of the family succession and of the paternal inheritance because of the Messianic promise that had been
made to Eve and had been reiterated to Sarah. About these
things Esau did not care. At an early age, Jacob recognized
their value and learned that life had a purpose. Hence it was
inevitable that family rivalry between the one who inherited
the blessing and did not value it and the one who did not
inherit it but did value it, should ensue. We all know the story
of Jacob's purchase of Esau's birthright for a mess of pottage.
The New Testament says in warning to professors of Christianity, "Lest there be any fornicator or profane person such as
Esau who for one morsel of meat sold his birthright. For ye
know how that afterward when he would have inherited the
blessing, he was rejected for he found no place of repentance
though he sought it carefully with tears" (Heb. 12:16, 17).
Jacob was exceedingly clever in the timing of his offer and in
appealing to Esau's weakest point, but nevertheless it was a
transaction by which the young son acquired the right of the
patriarchal blessing that belonged to the elder son. The Scripture places the responsibility upon Esau, for he treated it as of
no importance and of no value. Later, when Isaac was growing old, Esau sought to obtain the blessing because he then

understood its value, but that did not invalidate the contract into which he had entered with Jacob. Hence Jacob again stooped to get what he thought was now his own and by deception he received the patriarchal blessing. Both men were wrong. God had said that Jacob was chosen, but how God would have brought it about in His own good time we are not told. Even though Jacob deserved the blessing, we make no excuse for his use of deception in receiving it. Then with bitter cries and tears, Esau sought it with repentance but to no avail (Gen. 27: 34-40).

The smouldering quarrel now broke out into the open and became too strong to keep both sons in one household. Esau plotted to murder Jacob, which is another mark of the type of character found in Esau. The word of his plan came to Rebecca's ears, so she determined to save Jacob and also at the same time to get him a wife of the kind God required. She decided to send him to her kinspeople in Haran until Esau's anger had cooled. Her punishment in participating in the deception of the weak and aged Isaac was that she never saw her beloved and favorite son again. He departed for a twenty year sojourn, and ere he returned she had died. The Scripture implies that Jacob's departure was sudden, without taking leave of Esau. Isaac's agreement to it was gained by Rebecca, and without any personal attendants, and with little preparation, Jacob departed. What loneliness, fear, and discouragement beset his pathway by the time he had made one day's journey and rested at Bethel is revealed in that old hymn, which tells the story:

> *Though like the wanderer,*
> *The sun gone down,*
> *Darkness be over me,*
> *My rest a stone;*
> *Yet in my dreams I'd be*
> *Nearer, my God to Thee,*
> *Nearer to Thee.*

There let the way appear,
Steps unto heaven;
All that Thou sendest me
In mercy given;
Angels to beckon me
Nearer, my God, to Thee,
Nearer to Thee.

Then, with my waking thoughts,
Bright with Thy praise,
Out of my stony griefs,
Bethel I'll raise;
So by my woes to be
Nearer, my God, to Thee,
Nearer to Thee.

II. THE STORY OF THEIR IDYLLIC LOVE

Jacob and Rachel met at the old well in Haran. In the Near Eastern countries, courtship does not take place as it does here in the West. Here we want to be alone to speak our words in secret. There courtship is made in the open and usually at the well. Thus it was that Moses won his wife by a well in Midian. Jacob had completed his long journey by foot from Canaan and now was ready to rest by the well of Haran (Gen. 29). As he approached it, he saw three flocks waiting to be watered. He greeted two of the men who were the shepherds of two flocks, saying, "Know ye Laban the son of Nahor?" and they replied, "We know him." Jacob asked, "Is he well?" They replied, "He is well and behold Rachel his daughter cometh with the sheep." As yet Jacob could not see Rachel distinctly, so he told them to water their sheep, and they replied, "We cannot until all the flocks be gathered together, until they roll the stone from the well's mouth," and thus it was evident that a huge slab of rock was used to keep the well from all defilement.

By this time, Rachel arrived with her father's sheep, for she was a shepherdess. Then are written these important words, "When Jacob saw Rachel." When he saw her, it was love at first sight. Jacob simply fell all over himself to please her. Empowered by such a desire, he performed a feat of great strength in rolling the stone away from the well. Then he watered Rachel's entire flock as an act of gallantry while these strangers looked on. Finally, he picked her up and kissed her. The Scripture adds, "And he wept." Rachel must have reminded him of his mother, of home and all that he had left behind, and the lonely man wept for joy to find a relative of his mother and especially a woman such as Rachel.

This love of Jacob, which was born at the well, never changed through his long life. Some men are gallant and loving before marriage but soon forget it afterward. It was not so with Jacob. His love increased with the passing days and years. Jacob never had an eye for anyone else than for Rachel. Undoubtedly Rachel changed in appearance in the hard experiences of her primitive life, and she did not always look as fresh and appealing as she did that day by the well, but Rachel always remained the light of Jacob's eyes. When as an old man in Egypt, Jacob came to his last sickness and was speaking his final words to Joseph, he referred to Rachel, saying, "As for me, when I came from Padan, Rachel died by me in the land of Canaan in the way, when yet there was but a little way to come to Ephrath, and I buried her there in the way of Bethlehem" (Gen. 48:7). The memory of every deed and act of Rachel was fresh in the old man's mind. His love was undiminished.

A beautiful courtship followed this first love of Jacob for Rachel. Rachel hurriedly told her father Laban of the coming of Jacob, and at his invitation he abode with them for one month. What a month that must have been—attending Rachel as she cared for the sheep, the passing of evenings of sweet fellowship in the desert moonlight, and the enjoyment of pleasant conversations round the family hearth! At the end of the month, which passed like a day, Jacob asked Laban for the hand of his daughter and offered to serve for her for seven years as Laban's servant. Jacob could think of nothing better than living in this household as a hired servant if he could be in the presence of his beloved Rachel. The Scripture passes over those seven years in one sentence by saying, "They seemed unto him but a few days for the love he had to her" (Gen. 29:20). Here is scope for a great story, but it must be left to your imagination as you think of the kind of relationship that would make toil, such as that which Jacob later claimed that he endured, namely, sleep departing from him, being bitten by the frost, wandering by night and by day in order to protect the sheep, so easy that seven years seemed as seven days. Here is a demonstration of what love will enable a man to endure for a wife and for a home and for the object of his desire.

At the end of that season, a great wrong was done to Jacob by his future father-in-law. The marriage day arrived, the great eastern feast had been enjoyed, and it was time for Jacob to take his wife, when he discovered the base trick that had been played upon him through the means of veiling these eastern women. He had been given Rachel's sister, Leah, in marriage. One wonders why Jacob did not furiously demand his rightful wife and take her away. The only explanation of Jacob's submission to this wrong was that he recognized it as retribution for his own act of cheating Esau and deceiving his aged father. Jacob was compelled to serve another seven years for Rachel. Whether he was married at the beginning or at the end of these seven years is not quite clear from the Scriptural narrative, but at length marriage came. Jacob could not get along without Rachel; so he served fourteen years of his life to possess her (Gen. 29:26-30).

Now that marriage has occurred, we ought to look at the woman whom Jacob loved. Rachel certainly had her faults. One commentator calls her a soulless beauty, who thought only of self. We cannot agree with this, although no one can read the story of Rachel's life without recognizing her blemishes; but who is there who has not some blemishes in his character? From the beginning, Rachel was jealous of Leah, but why should she not be? She had been wronged as much by Laban's effrontery and Leah's connivance in it as had Jacob. If ever there was an argument against polygamy, it is this story. There simply could not be happiness in a household in which the affections and interests were divided between two women. As to Jacob's willingness to practice polygamy, we must make our judgment from the nature of the times in which he lived, in the lack of civil law, and from the absence of religious law upon his life. Second, Rachel was superstitious. When Jacob and his family and hers finally left Haran for Canaan after a twenty-one years' sojourn, Rachel took her father's teraphim, or idols, with her. According to the revelation made to Abraham, to Isaac, and to Jacob concerning the true God, this was idolatry and ultimately it had to be purged from Jacob's household. Third, Rachel was petulant. God had withheld children from her, and she blamed Jacob for it. How strange that in the case of so many mothers of the Bible who had great children their offspring were withheld from them until they reached an advanced age! Such was the case with Hannah, with the wife of Manoah, with Sarah, and with Elizabeth. One writer suggests that the purpose of this was to develop faith in them.

There were many favorable aspects to Rachel's character, as well as faults. She was not only attractive to Jacob, but she was a helpful, devoted wife under the most trying circumstances. She shared with Jacob most of his tests without complaint. There is also no shadow or stain over Rachel's virtuous life. She was an upright woman. Probably the greatest thing that can be attributed to her is that she was the mother of the mightiest of the patriarchs, who was great in faith and character, namely, Joseph. As one studies the life of Joseph and recognizes the purity of his character, he realizes that it must have had its source in his mother. When Rachel died, she was mourned by all who knew her and was crowned with many benedictions. Thus it is in the marriage ceremony that we pray, "God make you like Jacob and Rachel." No fault of Rachel diminished the love Jacob bore her. Here at least we see a wonderful figure of how Christ loves His church in spite of her faults. That means that He loves you in spite of the blemishes in your character, if you are a member of His church.

III. Their Life Together

There is only one hint of a jar in the harmonious relationship between Rachel and Jacob. The old adage says, "The course of true love never did run smooth." Sometime, somewhere, your perfect human relationship will be momentarily spoiled. This strain on the family tie was due to a commendable desire on the part of Rachel for children. Recall how the Scripture says that when Peninah, one wife of Elkanah, had children, and Hannah, another wife of Elkanah, had no children, that her adversary provoked her sorely to fret over this (I Sam. 1:6). Thus it was with Rachel. Her whole being was bound up in the thought of becoming a mother, and this desire ultimately became the cause of her death. To Jacob she said, "Give me children or I die." Jacob responded, "Am I in the stead of God?" and his anger was momentarily kindled against her, but it did not last long. Jacob could not continue angry with Rachel. It simply is not possible to cherish anger and reproach against one whom you love. The essence of love is that you forgive.

The time came when these two perennial lovers were to be separated by death. Here we catch the first glimpse in the Scripture of the price a woman pays for children. It is true that some because of joy that a child is born into the world refuse to admit sorrow, but terrible suffering is the lot of all women who become mothers, and some suffer even unto death. If it is true in natural life that woman must pass through the valley and the shadow of death if children are to be born, why should this not also be true in the spiritual life? It is true, for except Zion travail, her children will not be born. Converts to Christ are won through the suffering of the church. Rachel's time evidently came early, while she was traveling to Bethlehem as the Virgin Mary later did. The Scripture says, "She had hard labor." Finally, the attendant laid the little baby boy in her arms. Rachel was able to summon only enough strength to respond, "Child of my sorrow," before she passed away (Gen. 35;16-18). This name, "Benoni," was a prophecy by Rachel of the sufferings of her people. Like a ray of faith breaking over her last moments, she looked into the future and saw what Israel and the Church must bear. Centuries later, Jeremiah heard the voice and said, "Thus saith the Lord; A voice was heard in Rama, lamentation and bitter weeping; Rachel weeping for her children and refused to be comforted for her children because they were not" (Jer. 31:15). When Herod slaughtered the innocents, the word of Jeremiah was again fulfilled in the crying of the mothers (Matt. 2:18), and thus Rachel stands as an example of suffering motherhood before the whole world, and thus we honor her.

The effect on Jacob of the passing of Rachel was disastrous. It brought a grief from which he never fully recovered even till his death. Some people seem to be able to brush aside the loss of a loved one in a few weeks. Not so with Jacob. Jacob went about his regular duties of life, but now and then he let fall a word that revealed that he had buried his heart in that tomb on the road to Bethlehem, a tomb which remains to our present day. After the death of Rachel, Jacob transferred his love to her children. Whenever he saw them, he remembered the lovely dark-eyed daughter of Laban. Thus we hear the story of Joseph and the coat of many colors given by Jacob because of the love for him. Thus we hear the new name of Rachel's last child now called "Benjamin," or "son of my right hand," by Jacob, for by these two children Jacob now set his store. It is no wonder that a controversy arose between the ten other sons of Jacob and these two, and that when Joseph had been sold into Egypt and the ten sons had returned from their first visit to him as the unrecognized governor of Egypt, demanding that Benjamin be taken also, Jacob said, "My son shall not go down . . . if mischief befall him . . . then shall ye bring down my gray hairs with sorrow to the grave" (Gen. 42:38). Finally, when word came to Jacob that Joseph was still alive, the Bible says, "The spirit of Jacob their father revived and Israel said, It is enough. Joseph my son is yet alive.

I will go and see him before I die" (Gen. 45:28). From being called Jacob, which means supplanter, we now have a man called Israel, which means the prince of God, a transformation which was wrought through suffering brought to him through his love for Rachel. He had been made to limp through life because he had wrestled with an angel; he had recognized the sins of his youth returning to him in his age; and he was lifted to a life of worthiness to be the progenitor of the Christ, through love.

We only call your attention to the following lessons: First, that Jacob represents Israel dispersed and suffering and by means of suffering ultimately brought back to God. Second, Jacob may be made to represent Christ, who loved His church to the end. What meaning this holds for every believer who is a part of His bride! Third, Benoni, or "Son of my sorrow," re-echoes in the New Testament experience of the bride of Christ. The church will have suffering in this world, but it will be united with Him in love forever. Thus it is written, "If we suffer with Him, we shall also be glorified together." Benoni will become Benjamin, "Son of my right hand."

4

Miriam

THE WOMAN WHO HELPED LEAD A NATION

*And Miriam the prophetess . . . took a timbrel in her hand;
and all the women went out after her . . . And Miriam
answered them, Sing ye unto the Lord, for he hath tri-
umphed gloriously* (Ex. 15:20,21).

Miriam belonged to a notable family in Israel (Num.
26:59). Her mother's name was Jochebed and she was one of
the most remarkable characters in Scripture. This mother in
Israel imparted her faith to her children. The only explanation
of Moses' "choosing rather to suffer affliction with the people
of God, than to enjoy the pleasures of sin for a season" lies in
the training which his mother gave to him (Heb. 11:24). The
fact that Moses, after being trained for years in the court of
Pharaoh, would renounce the position of a son to Pharaoh's
daughter, or heir to the throne, and identify himself with the
Hebrew slave people was due to the faith that was imparted
to him by his mother. It was her instruction which governed
the lives of Aaron, Miriam and Moses. Miriam and Aaron had
been born before the edict of Pharaoh to kill the male children,
but Moses lived in the days when the victims were being
killed and he was only saved through the faith of his mother.
Jochebed's piety in the midst of the suffering of the Hebrews
was an example from which these children could never escape.

Amram, the husband of Jochebed, was an unknown Levite,
unhonored, unsung and unrecorded in Scripture save for the
one reference in Numbers 26:59. Probably he was a faithful,
loyal, diligent servant of Jehovah but exhausted in the slavery

43

to which the Hebrew people were subject in Egypt. He had no time or energy to rise above the animal life of endless labor, eating, sleeping and reproducing. The days of the Egyptian bondage were very hard and the service to which he was subject rigorous.

The three children were Aaron, Moses and Miriam. Aaron and Moses were great brothers and leaders in Israel, Aaron, eight years Moses' senior, was without any special education except what Amram and Jochebed could give to him in the midst of their environmental limitation. But Aaron was gifted with a facile speech. To Moses God said, "I know that your brother Aaron can speak." Aaron was something of a born leader, resourceful and independent, taking his place of prominence in spite of lack of education. Moses is described as exceedingly fair and promising from birth and was destined to be the greatest man in the Old Testament and one of the truly great men of history. Miriam, who was the oldest of the children, had her share of great qualities in the most unusual family. She was a spinster who was the first true mother of a nation. Due to the stress through which the nation was passing in its slavery, she forewent the privilege of marriage.

By way of analogy, one could look back to a great American family of similar influence. I speak of Lyman Beecher who was father of the remarkable family composed of Edward Beecher, a pastor of Park Street Church, Henry Ward Beecher, the famous preacher, Harriet Beecher Stowe, the author of *Uncle Tom's Cabin*, and Catherine Beecher, the spinster school teacher. The influence of this family in the mid-nineteenth century was incalculable.

MIRIAM'S SUPERVISION OF THE INFANT MOSES

The book of Exodus begins with a description of the sufferings of the Hebrews as a slave people in Egypt. They made their advent into Egypt under Joseph who had been sold into bondage, who had risen to the second in power in the nation, and who during the famine in the middle east had invited his father and eleven brethren, with their families, to settle in

the fertile land of Goshen. There they had multiplied excee_
ingly over the years. Then, as the decades passed, there arose
"a Pharaoh who knew not Joseph." This Biblical statement
describes a change in the dynasties of Egypt. During the days
of Joseph and the early residence of the Israelites in Egypt,
the Hyksos, a Semitic people, were ruling over Egypt. The
Hebrews were related to the Hyksos and thus received favorable consideration. In the due process of time, however, the
Egyptians from the south of Egypt, or upper reaches of the
Nile, reconquered the lower Egypt and expelled the Hyksos.
Fearing that the Hebrews would be a pocket of treason, they
enslaved them. Out of fear of the Hebrews, they attempted to
reduce their numbers by killing the male children at birth. The
rest of the nation was subjected to ruthless exploitation in the
building of treasure cities called Ramses and Pithom. During
these days of duress and stress, it seems the impression was
made upon Miriam that it would be better not to be married
than to bring children into the world who would either be
killed, or be enslaved, or be subject to such stress. A similar
situation existed during the New Testament in which Paul
advised the virgins to remain unmarried during the time of
stress (I Cor. 7:26). Miriam was a woman who had dedicated
herself to her family and to the needs of her people. She was
one of a long train of women who have done this as nurses,
teachers, servants and missionaries. Praise should be upon the
lips of all men for those single women who had dedicated
themselves to the service of humanity. Legion is their number.

In the midst of these sufferings of the Hebrews, culminating in the slaying of their young children, the child Moses was
born and saved (Ex. 2:1-10). One can imagine the mingled
faith and fear which was experienced in the home of Amram
and Jochebed. Their faith was exhibited in their determination to save this unusually fair and beautiful child. But as the
days and weeks passed on, Moses grew, and they were smitten
with fear. Every time an Egyptian soldier marched down the
cobblestone streets, or an Egyptian commoner passed by, the
child Moses was hidden, now among the sheaves, now in the

deep chimney, now amid the produce, while unspoken prayers lay upon the lips of the mother and imminent danger heightened the tension of the family on every side. Finally, necessity dictated that some escape should be had. Jochebed's faith was expressed in her resorting to the device of making an ark of bulrushes in which to place the child Moses and commit him to the Nile. The elements of hazard were great for the Nile was infested at certain parts with crocodiles and almost anything could happen to a child, depending on who discovered him. With care, however, she placed him in the Nile where the daughter of Pharaoh came with her maidens from time to time to bathe. Jochebed believed that God had a place in His providence for Moses and she was willing to commit the child unto that providence. Hence, the baby Moses was found by the daughter of Pharaoh. Nigh at hand, Jochebed had set Miriam, Moses' faithful twelve-year-old sister, to watch what would become of the babe. Never did a sister bear a more important watch than that, for in Moses was tied up the future of the Israelitish people. Seeing the ark, Pharaoh's daughter commanded it to be brought to her, and when it was opened she saw the beautiful boy Moses, who responded with crying and touched the heart of the woman. Immediately, Miriam made her way, with wisdom, into the group and suggested that she go and find a Hebrew nurse for the child for it was obvious that this was one of the Hebrew children that had been commanded to be killed. The suggestion was seized upon by Pharaoh's daughter, Miriam was dispatched for a nurse, and she brought back Jochebed, Moses' own mother, to nurse him. Hence, in the providence of God, Moses was not only spared but his mother was paid wages for being his nurse, was given security in the rearing of her child and opportunity to inculcate in him the faith which was later expressed in his life.

Supervision of Moses' boyhood was probably committed largely to his sister, Miriam. The slaves were compelled to work long hours and unless Jochebed's part in that slavery was mitigated by order of Pharaoh's daughter, she, too, was compelled to bear great burdens. Just as the younger children are committed to the older children for care in the Orient today, so Moses was committed unto Miriam. Hence, she developed a sense of responsibility for Moses, of importance to Moses, and a closeness with Moses during these formative years of his life.

Then came the day when Moses was separated from the family and taken to the palace where he was formally adopted as the son of Pharaoh's daughter. This meant that he was to be educated in all the learning of the Egyptians which had reached a great height as exhibited in the construction of the pyramids, in the mathematical systems, in the intricate dentistry as evidenced in the mummies and in relics in the museums in Egypt today. It also meant that Moses would be trained as a soldier and as a ruler. Tradition says that he was a general in the Egyptian army and took his place of leadership in the empire.

Miriam's Support of Moses' Leadership

We are now transported over several decades to the time of the exodus. Miriam had passed through much during the interim. She had been twelve years of age at Moses' birth, had been in her late teens when Moses had been taken to be trained, and she had suffered affliction with the people of God in Egypt during the entire interim until the time of the exodus. This was the worst season of Israel's history. God says that their cry arose to Him by reason of their bondage. He had seen the cruelty with which they were being treated, the beatings which they underwent, the sighings from their weariness and sorrows, and God had come down to deliver them. He had appeared unto Moses in the wilderness and said: "Come now, I will send you unto Pharaoh." During this time Miriam had achieved a place of leadership in Israel. She had encouraged her people during their sufferings.

Already she had seen God do much. There was that day when He had visited Aaron and commanded him to go forth into the wilderness to meet his brother Moses whom He had

called to be a deliverer of Israel. She had seen Moses and
Aaron return unto Egypt, greet the elders of the slave people,
rehearse before them the divine commission, and show them
the signs which God had given of their mission. These supernatural certifications were sufficient to convince the Israelites.
What thrills must have passed over Miriam as her dreams of
deliverance of the people of Israel began to come true. How
often she had said, "If only I were a man! I would rally this
people and show these Egyptians a thing or two." Perhaps in
Moses' boyhood she had even suggested such ideas to him.
Miriam was a woman like Deborah, like Joan of Arc.

With inspired interest she had watched the various stages
in the contest between Moses and Pharaoh. She knew of his
demands to let the people go to worship God in the wilderness
and the haughty refusal of Pharaoh which resulted in the increase of their burdens. She passed through the days when in
response to God's commands Moses had stretched forth his rod
over Egypt and the various plagues had come which had almost
totally decimated and destroyed the land. She had participated
in the passover, had placed the blood upon the posts of the
door, had eaten of the paschal lamb and then had heard the
wail which had arisen over Egypt in the death of the firstborn.
She had followed Moses and Aaron as they left Egypt, leading
the people of Israel, their cattle, their possessions and the
goods which they had expropriated from Egypt in haste.

She had watched the cloud by day and the pillar of fire
by night as it had separated the Israelites from the hosts of
Pharaoh who had followed seeking to overcome these Israelites.
And finally, she had seen Moses stretch his rod out over the
Red Sea which under a strong east wind had divided, rolling
back the walls of water on the right and the left so that the
Israelites could march through upon dry ground. Afterwards,
when the Egyptians had assayed to do the same, she saw
Moses stretch forth his rod again on the eastern bank of the
Red Sea and the walls of water break down and inundate
these Egyptian hosts. It was a frightening, amazing and stu-
pendous miracle.

In all this Miriam had taken part, for she is called "a prophetess" (Ex. 15:20). God had been speaking to the Israelites through Miriam across the years that had passed. This was not an unsual phenomenon according to the Old Testament, but here was the first prophetess. She maintained her position as the leader of the women of Israel and as a spokesman of God to the nation. Now, at the conclusion of the passing of this great people through the Red Sea as on dry ground, she led the ecstatic dances of the women in the wilderness as they sang the song of Moses. (Ex. 15:20,21). No one had a more exalted place in Israel's history than Miriam. The song which Moses wrote and which they rehearsed in full throat and power is recorded in Exodus 15:1-18. It is a song of victory, of the power of God, of the defeat of God's enemies and of the triumph of faith. In Revelation 15:3 we are told that it is the song of Moses which will be sung by the redeemed when they experience their great victory over the beast at the end of the ages. Thus, Miriam participated in the leadership of Moses and sustained him and supported him throughout his struggles.

MIRIAM'S SIN OF REVOLT AGAINST MOSES

Because Miriam's sin is illustrative of what may happen to any believer, let him who stands take heed lest he fall. The sense of pique which inspired Miriam's revolt against Moses was caused by the arrival of Moses' Cushite wife on the scene after the exodus. This woman is called an "Ethiopian woman" (Num. 12:1-5). There is some debate as to the identity of this person. The question is whether Moses took unto himself a second wife, or whether this was the appearance on the scene of Zipporah, the daughter of Reuel, who was a Midianite. Midian was a descendant of Abraham by Keturah, his second wife, after the death of Sarah. Among the Midianites were pockets of the old Cushites, or descendents of Ham who had not all migrated from Egypt or Africa. Some think that Moses had a second marriage here; others think that this was merely the appearance of Zipporah. If the woman is to be identified with Zipporah, then she was not necessarily black, but may have been. Zipporah had two sons by Moses, Gershom and Eliezer, and she was not a believer for she resented the covenant and the sign of the circumcision (Exod. 4:19-28).

If it was Zipporah that appeared among the Israelites at this time, then we understand how the attention of the people was transferred to her. She became the first lady, receiving the deference, honor and consideration of the people of Israel. This was more than Miriam could stand and it became the occasion of her revolt against the authority of Moses. Miriam began to manifest jealousy, then envy, and then revolt. She blamed Moses for the appearance of Zipporah. She criticized him to Aaron, claiming that he took unto himself too great an authority, and she started a whispering campaign that broke out into open revolt. The Scripture summarizes it by the question, "Hath the Lord indeed spoken only by Moses?" Had we been able to overhear what was said within the tents of Israel in those days, we could have listened to backbiting, suspicion and accusation. Miriam stirred up Aaron to express what was in his own heart, for there was cause enough for Aaron also to be jealous of his brother Moses. There is enough evil in all of us to be susceptible of this. Jealousy, avarice, lust, lurks within the heart of every human being.

But Miriam was punished for touching the Lord's anointed. In all of the whispering that went on, Moses manifested a true spirit of faith and submission. He had heard and seen it all but had said nothing. The Scripture says, "Now the man Moses was very meek, above all the men which were upon the face of the earth" (Num. 12:3). In Moses' attitude he displayed the New Testament characteristic of committing one's way unto the Lord and allowing vengeance to come from God alone (Rom. 12:16). By taking such a position and patiently enduring the slights, offenses and heartaches to which his wife and he were subject, Moses allowed the Lord to work. Hence, the Lord spoke suddenly unto Moses, Aaron and Miriam, saying, "Come out ye three unto the tabernacle of the congregation." There God expressed His commendation of

Moses, rebuked Miriam, expressed His anger, and departed. As the cloud went up from the tabernacle, Aaron and Moses received the terrible shock of looking upon Miriam and finding that she was leprous. Little did Aaron know but what he also was leprous when he looked into his sister's face because he had shared in the revolt although she had instigated it. He cried out unto Moses to intercede, which Moses did, but the Lord commanded that she be thrust out of the camp for seven days. Thus, as a leper, Miriam went out to join the outcasts, with her head uncovered, her lips covered, with the necessity of crying out, "Unclean," to all who came, to live in loneliness amid those barren hills outside the camp. What burdens she bore and what heartache as she watched the campfires of Israel by night and as she sat in the loneliness of those days!

Aaron had had the onerous duty of shutting his sister Miriam outside the camp although he had participated in her sin. Little did he know but what she might forever be shut out from Israel. We may be sure that from that day on Aaron had a new sympathy for lepers. Moses had turned to God saying, "Heal her now, O God, I beseech thee." God had smitten Miriam and God was to heal Miriam, forgiving her for Moses' sake, but she was not allowed to enter the camp for seven days, at which time Aaron had to examine her and pronounce her clean. During those seven days the entire Israelite encampment paused and a pall of sadness rested upon it as it realized that a great leader had fallen.

The next and final reference to Miriam is in Numbers 20:1. It speaks about her death. We do not know exactly how long it was before Miriam died, but it is certain that she lost her place of leadership. She had no further part in public events. She had learned her lesson. No doubt the rest of her days were spent in laboring for the outcasts, assisting the lepers, feeding those who were stricken, for she was through with public life.

This noble woman, like all of us, had a point of weakness to which she succumbed, but which also she conquered.

5

Rahab

The Woman Who Discovered the Power of Faith

> And she said unto the men, As soon as we heard these
> things, our hearts did melt, neither did there remain any
> more courage in any man, because of you: for the Lord
> your God, he is God in heaven above, and in the earth
> beneath (Josh. 2:9,11).

There is a higher morality in life than that of personal virtue. It is the morality of atonement and it is based upon faith in what God has done. Herein lies the great hope for all sinners who may be justified or declared righteous before the tribunal of God, before they have any personal righteousness or any meritorious standing. Rahab is a fine illustration of this great Biblical truth of the higher morality.

Rahab was a base strumpet, a harlot, a woman who sub mitted to any man who crossed her threshold for sinful purposes, who sold her body for money, and who practiced what has been called "the oldest profession in the world." Ethically and morally speaking, Rahab was anything but the kind of woman one would expect to be singled out as an example in a matter of religious standing.

Rahab was delivered from her sin and given a place with Sarah in the roster of the heroes of the faith, who were justified and declared righteous (Heb. 11:31). It seems incredible that Rahab should take her place with Abel, Enoch, Noah, Abraham, Sarah, Moses and the other heroes of the faith, and yet she does. She was given this position not after she reformed, but while she was still a harlot. This seems all the more in-

congruous and yet it sets forth the principle about which we are speaking in a very clear light.

Rahab was inducted or adopted into the family of the Israelites. She married a prince in Israel, by name Salmon, and she became one of the progenitors of the sinless one, namely, Jesus Christ (Matt. 1:5). The incongruity of this is seen in the attempt by some interpreters to avoid the embarrassment by making the Hebrew word mean, "a landlady" or "a formerly fallen woman," etc. They try to circumvent the direct meaning of the word "harlot," but the very fact of Rahab's sinful condition is the glory of this message. Hence, this should teach us something about the nature of saving faith.

The Startling Discovery of Faith

In the story of Rahab we see faith exhibited in an inhospitable environment, in an immoral woman and in an impending catastrophe, all of which surprises us.

The environment in which Rahab lived was the Amorite civilization centering in Jericho. These Amorites worshiped Chemosh, Milcom, Baal and Asteroth. These were brutal, vengeful and lustful heathen deities. The worship of Chemosh demanded the offering up of children as living sacrifices to the god and the passing through fire on the part of devotees. The worship of Baal and Asteroth involved immortality. These were fertility deities and they inspired the corruption of a people. The old adage "as gods, as people," applied to the Amorites. The people rise no higher than the gods they worship. If there are immorality and lascivious relationships and vengeful acts in the legends of the gods, the people excuse themselves for practicing similar acts.

We are not in the dark about the morality of these Amorite peoples. Since the discovery of the Ugaritic tablets at Ras Shamra the condition of the Amorite civilization is plainly known. About this we read, "The myths and practices described in this unique collection of documents reflect the most frightful barbarism and abound in magic rites of gods and demigods that are stupefying, primitive, gross and sensual.

Particular significance is attached to the rites of the goddess of fertility. The other nations of the old world also worshiped goddesses of fertility, anchoring the cycles of growth and decay, of birth and death to their ritual. But in Canaan they were openly shameless. Mother goddesses were, for example, branded as 'holy whores'. . . .

"The goddesses of fertility were worshiped principally on hills and knolls. Their votaries erected for them Asherim and set out 'sacred pillars' or trees under which the rites were practiced." Compare I Kings 14:23.

As a result of these religious practices the decadence of the people became complete. It was this corruption and iniquity of the Canaanites which God promised to destroy. He said to Abraham, "The iniquity of the Amorites is not yet full" (Gen. 15:16). Four hundred years later when the Israelites invaded Canaan, the cup of iniquity was full and God commanded them to exterminate these corrupt and wicked people. When Jericho was destroyed, it was placed under a special curse of desolation (Josh. 6:26). For us to think of a woman of faith in the midst of this corruption is quite surprising.

Moreover, we find faith in an immoral woman. Rahab desecrated her body to commercial uses. How she began this sinful practice, we know not. Probably she fell by the usual means: either temptation, or seduction, or perfidy, or force, or alcohol; but whatever the original cause, that first fall was long past and she now lived by means of the prostituting of her body. Hers was the habitual resort to immorality to earn a living. Recently there have been revelations over radio, on television and in the newspapers of similar practices which are going on in the United States. The extent of this practice was shocking and challenging. Students of history know that prostitution has had a place in the life of all peoples, but there is evidence that America today is surpassing in the depth of degradation even the worst periods of history. The house that Rahab maintained was a house of prostitution so marked and so known in Jericho. She conducted her evil house with the connivance of the authorities as is done even today.

Rahab was held in disdain by society. Even in a civilization which practices immorality in its religious rites and maintained temple priestesses who were harlots, a woman like Rahab who made her living by this means was ostracized. It is obvious from the narrative that she was separated from her family and was considered an untouchable. The fact that prostitution becomes a general practice does not remove the stigma from those who are engaged in it. Society exacts a price of ostracism for such.

We may believe that Rahab had a basic desire for a better life. She had no satisfaction in the worship of Jericho's filthy gods, or in the measure of security which she seemed to get from her business. There was in her a deep yearning for something better and from traveling merchants who used her house on the wall for the dual purpose of an inn and of indulgence, she heard the reports of what had happened to the people of Israel in Egypt and during their wanderings in the wilderness. She knew all about the dividing of the Red Sea and the catastrophe which overtook the Egyptians. She heard about the successful wars which Israel had waged against the people on the other side of Jordan. She knew about the miracles which God had performed for this people and as she heard of these things, hope sprang in her heart that this God might be the answer to her own spiritual problems. Such a hope alone can explain her subsequent action. Her hope was based upon a faith in the God of Israel as she later testified to the spies.

Rahab's faith was displayed in the midst of an impending catastrophe. The time of judgment for the Amorites and for Jericho was imminent. Rahab must have sensed this. Any spiritually sensitive soul today can sense the intimation in our own civilization that judgment is near. We are hearing admonitions of this from military men, diplomats, educators and ecclesiastical leaders. Even the scientists are adding their voice to the chorus. Rahab lived in a time of despair rather than a time of faith and hope. Yet, strange to say, in that despairing time hope was born within her heart. This is to say that there are times of catastrophe which produce faith. One can never tell in what area faith will arise. Beauty is often found in unexpected places. Friendship sometimes blooms in the midst of hostility. Thus, we understand the startling nature of this faith in Rahab.

The Surprising Deeds of Faith

Rahab immediately recognized these two Jewish spies as members of the foreign and invading Israelites, yet she received them into her home. This act is called by James a justifying work (James 2:25). It was an act which grew out of her faith and demonstrated her faith. James makes it parallel to Abraham's being justified by his willingness to offer Isaac on the altar. In both cases the works grew out of their faith.

Rahab's act constituted treason. She immediately recognized the men as those who had come to spy out the land for the purpose of conquest (Josh. 2:2). Had Rahab been discovered harboring, protecting and aiding the escape of these spies, no mercy would have been shown to her by the king of Jericho. Rahab must have immediately sensed the difference between these men who came to seek refuge in her home and those who came for a sinful purpose. They became the messengers of God to her. It was possible for God to convert her without the instrumentality of these spies, but according to the Bible God uses means in order to bring people to a faith in Him. Hence, we may believe that when Rahab made it known to them that she recognized who they were, they preached to her and answered her questions. She was even able to comfort them in their fear of what could happen to them by her faith in the God of Israel who had done wonders, who had made the land to tremble before them, and who is the God of heaven and of earth (Josh. 2:9-11).

Rahab decided for the God of Israel. She confessed her faith in God over against all the gods of the Amorites. She said, "For the Lord your God, he is God in heaven above, and in earth beneath." On this ground, she asked for mercy to be

extended to herself, to her parents, and to her family, for she
believed that the God of the Israelites would deliver Jericho
into their hands. Thus, Rahab committed herself to the deliverance of these Israelites at the peril of her own life. She
took them to the roof of her house and hid them in the stalks
of flax. This flax undoubtedly was used for making linen and
occupied Rahab during certain hours of the day and sup-
plemented her income. Rahab then lied unto the emissaries
who were sent by the king to discover the men who had been
seen to enter her home. It would have been an easy thing for
her to inform on these spies, to have them turned over to the
king of Jericho, and to have thus participated in their death.
However, Rahab took her stand with them and delivered them.
Rahab thus illustrates how important it is to act upon the
knowledge which one possesses. To wait, to toy with the possibilities, to debate over the knowledge of the Gospel is to lose
one's opportunity. She heard the Word, she saw the opportunity and she acted. Her decision was fraught with great consequences and so is the decision of every man who faces the
content of the Gospel.

Rahab's faith was demonstrated by her intercession for
her family. This was the first evidence of her changed life
(Josh. 2:13). Rahab had been separated from her parents and
family probably due to her profession, yet she immediately
forgave this separation and condemnation and sought their
salvation. She did not want to be saved alone. She had a burden for her family. This is evidence of a true conversion. When
an individual finds the forgiveness of his own sins and his own
deliverance, he immediately begins to think of others and the
natural thing is to begin with his own family. In this, Rahab
is an example of what happens to every saved sinner. A
prominent New Testament example of this is the conversion of
Matthew after which he immediately gave a dinner to all his
former publicans and friends at which he introduced Jesus to
them as his Saviour. This was the time when Matthew made
his clean break with his former profession and began to follow
the Saviour. No one is truly saved who does not immediately

feel the burden for and desire for the salvation of those with whom he formerly practiced his sin.

Thus, the covenant made with Rahab by these spies was extended to her family. All who were in her house, marked by the scarlet cord, would be saved. This also is a Biblical truth. Paul said to the Philippian jailer, "Believe on the Lord Jesus Christ and thou shalt be saved, and thy house" (Acts 16:31). The Lord promises household salvation. The covenant position of believers even includes the unbelieving husband, or the unbelieving wife so that their children are holy (I Cor. 7:14). Hence, when we become converted and enter the covenant, it is our responsibility to get our families under the blood. Rahab went to them and witnessed of Israel's God and of the impending judgment. That she succeeded was evident in the fact that they took refuge within her house while the Israelites were marching around Jericho during the critical week. Her success should be compared with Lot's failure in Sodom. Lot was not able to win his sons-in-law and even members of his own family.

The Saving Destiny of Faith

Rahab was delivered from judgment. She was secure even in the most dangerous place during the attack of the Israelites upon Jericho. Her house was situated on the wall. The wall was the first structure to collapse at the time of the attack and yet, in the midst of the heat of the battle, Rahab's house was maintained and she was physically delivered by those whom she had harbored. Her family was gathered in that house. This is evidence of what a convincing evangelist she was during those few days between the departure of the spies and the fall of Jericho. These members of her family watched the Israelites through the window out of which the spies had escaped as they marched around the city of Jericho. Each day that multitude followed the priest around the town once. On the seventh day they marched around the town seven times. Possibly some of the members of the family cast mocking, slurring, unbelieving remarks concerning the Israelites, but Rahab's faith extended beyond the Israelites unto their God and that faith was exemplified by the red cord that floated from her window. She saw God in those hosts and through her faith came her salvation and the salvation of her family. The people of Jericho were exterminated but Rahab and her family were saved.

Rahab was also delivered from a sinful past. In the destruction of Jericho, Rahab's house of prostitution tumbled down never to be used again. In this event the career of corruption of Rahab was ended. She was sanctified by a faith which separated her from Jericho and identified her with Israel, the people of God. This was the beginning of a life of identification with the people of God. Rahab began a life of faith and purity which terminated in her marriage to Salmon (Matt. 1:5) who was probably one of the spies whom she had befriended.

By her faith Rahab was delivered from oblivion. No doubt there were many more virtuous women in Jericho and even in Israel of that generation than was Rahab, and yet they were buried unknown and unsung. However, the memory of Rahab is enshrined in the book of the heroes of the faith. She takes a noble place with Abel, Enoch, Noah, Abraham, Moses and David. More than this, she became an ancestress of the Lord Jesus Christ by her marriage to Salmon who was the ancestor of Boaz, who was the ancestor of David, who was the ancestor of Christ. Thus, through faith, Rahab experienced the fullness of deliverance.

Rahab stands as an evidence of salvation, of justification by faith. She believed when others did not. She chose the people of God and the God of Israel as her God. She dedicated her all to God and hazarded her very security upon this faith. She acted on her faith as we symbolized by the scarlet cord. Thus those who put their faith in the promise of salvation by the blood of Jesus Christ will find their security and their deliverance. Quite correctly the scarlet cord has stood for the atoning blood of our Lord Jesus Christ through which a sinner, while yet in his sins, may be forgiven, justified and regenerated so that out of that experience he may be a new creature, separated unto God and the people of God. Rahab will forever stand as an illustration and proof of the atonement as the higher morality established by God.

6

Delilah

The Woman Who Ruined a Holy Man

> *She made him sleep upon her knees; and she called for a man, and she caused him to shave off the seven locks of his head; and she began to afflict him, and his strength went from him* (Judg. 16:19).

There were many good women in the ancestry of Christ, but when the Holy Spirit singled out four of them to be included in His genealogy, whom did He choose? Sarah, Rachel, and the godly women? No. He chose Tamar, notorious for shameful fornication; Rahab, given to the abomination of harlotry; Ruth, a despised Moabitess who was forbidden access to the congregation; and Bathsheba, with whom David sinned. Herein we have illustrations of how the Lord saves through faith, delivers from natural punishment, and secures our salvation. We wish to emphasize this same redemptive process in singling out women of the Bible for study.

In this instance, we choose Delilah, *The Woman Who Ruined a Holy Man.* Let us look, first, at the man who was ruined, namely, Samson; second, at the woman who ruined him, namely, Delilah; and third, at the ruin which engulfed them both.

I. Samson, the Man Who Was Ruined

We have called Samson the man who was ruined. His life impresses us as one gigantic ruin. That it once was beautiful and effective for God there can be no doubt, for the Book of Hebrews enrolls him as one of the heroes of the faith of whom the world was not worthy. In him God had built a structure that was magnificent, but Samson himself brought it to ruin through the influence of a woman.

That Samson merits the title of a holy man is evident from the statement about his life. As with Isaac, Samuel, and John the Baptist, a supernatural element is connected with him in his birth. The angel of the Lord appeared unto the aged wife of Manoah with the promise, "Thou shalt conceive and bear a son" (Judg. 13). Later the annunciation was made to Manoah. The child was to be a supernatural gift of God to these righteous parents. The angel even went into detail as to the prenatal influences that would be brought to bear upon the son. The mother was to drink no wine nor strong drink and was to be exceedingly careful concerning unclean things mentioned in the Jewish Law.

It is significant that when God wants a man, He usually begins to prepare that man through his parents. If our own day is to produce leaders who are able to preserve our American heritage, it will be necessary for God to begin with the mothers and find some who will be separated unto His will before ever the children are born.

Manoah performed a sacrifice unto the angel and we read that the angel "did wondrously." He ascended into the sky in the presence of Manoah and his wife, and Manoah said, "We have seen the Lord." Undoubtedly this was none other than He whose name is called "Wonderful." In due time the child was born and they named him "Samson," or "Sunny," because of the light hair, ruddy complexion, and bright disposition of the boy. He was a joy to the hearts of his father and mother, who had longed for such a possession.

The angel had said, "The child shall be a Nazarite unto God from the womb." To take the vow of a Nazarite meant to separate oneself unto the Lord. The sign of this was that the individual partook of no wine or strong drink whatsoever; that he let his hair grow in seven locks, which were braided back of his head; and that he observed the laws concerning the defilement of the body. Note that when one was to be sanctified and separated unto the Lord he was to touch no liquor. The great generals of history, such as Caesar, Charlemagne, Gustavus Adolphus, Frederick the Great, Cromwell, and Napoleon, with the single exception of Alexander the Great, were men given to temperance. They knew that liquor and a clear head do not go together. If a man would be holy unto the Lord he must abstain from all use of liquor. Not only was the Nazarite, Samson, to abstain, but also his parents were commanded to abstain. The only adequate principle toward liquor is a total abstinence. John the Baptist was also a Nazarite, and the clearer picture of him in the common mind might help to clarify the indistinct picture of Samson. It was the custom of men such as Paul to take upon them a Nazarite vow for a particular length of time, but the Baptist and Samson were Nazarites from birth. The vow was a symbol of the consecration of an individual unto the Lord.

During Samson's youth, he was possessed of mighty strength and physical power. If the craven, degenerated, almost despicable Israelites of Samson's day had only seen what it would have meant to have been visited by the Spirit of the Lord and what God could have done with a nation so consecrated unto Him, they would not have been vassals of the Philistines and the Canaanites. Samson's strength was simply an evidence of a supernatural power given to him by God. Hence, during his youth, he made intermittent forays into the Philistines' country, playing huge jokes upon them and usually delivering himself by his cleverness and his great strength.

As a young man, it was evident that Samson was established to be a judge in Israel. He was a great deliverer, and he judged the nation for twenty years. Our knowledge of the conditions of the people are drawn from the Book of Judges, where it says, "Every man did that which was right in his own eyes" (Judg. 21:25). There, sodomy among the Benjamites caused the rest of the Israelites to wipe out the entire tribe with the exception of six hundred people. There, as craven slaves of the Philistines for nearly fifty years, the Israelites went down to the country of the Philistines to sharpen their instruments of agriculture. No swords were allowed in that nation. There the priests committed adultery with the women of the land. In the midst of these sons of Belial, Samson attempted to judge the nation on the basis of God's law. However, the promise made unto Manoah was that Samson should begin to deliver Israel. There is an implication here that he would not complete the deliverance, and he certainly did not. Under the Spirit of God, Samson constituted the only bulwark against the Philistines, who at that period had reached the height of their material prosperity and military strength. The degeneration of his own countrymen was shown when a thousand of them bound him on one occasion and turned him over to the Philistines instead of assisting him to deliver the country from the dominion of the Philistines. During those twenty years as judge of Israel, Samson was striving to do what was right. He was a symbol of self-control and of consecration. Though the sons of Belial waited for his halting, he alone walked with God in a position of power and holiness.

Samson's power was dependent entirely upon his obedience and his separation. The Lord had chosen Samson for a purpose. He had made a covenant with him before his birth, the sign of which was the Nazarite vow. The parents of Samson were righteous and godly people and not only rehearsed to him the conditions that were revealed to them before his birth, but they explained to him the meaning of the Nazarite vow and the need of Israel for a great deliverer in their day. Their hopes for this child were high, and they taught him to know the Lord and to observe his part of the conditions imposed by God's covenant.

At least the Spirit of God was upon him and enabled him to do great exploits. Samson was an example of the text, "they that know their God shall be strong and do exploits" (Dan. 11: 32). On one occasion he rent a lion as he would a kid. He alone composed an army able to defeat a thousand Philistines. He could lift up the gates of a city and carry them bodily up to the top of a hill and deposit them in scorn of the enemy. Samson was a man of riddles, one who jested with the enemy and who presumed on his own strength. Samson had to learn that it is "not by might nor by power" but by the Spirit of the Lord (Zech. 4:6).

Though there were many and wonderful things in the life of Samson, none of them are recorded for us, not even a single case that he judged in Israel; yet the story of his temptation and his weakness and his fall are presented to us in vivid language in order that they may be a warning to us. The point of Samson's weakness was women. Like Solomon, he loved many strange women, and they became a snare unto him (I Kings 11:1).

First, there was the case of the daughter of Timnath. On one of his expeditions into the country of the Philistines he saw a beautiful face and was lured by it. Quite often love leaps the boundaries of race, creed, and country, leading men into strange unions. Much to the consternation of his parents, on his return he asked that they get that woman for him. His parents remonstrated, saying, "Is there never a woman among the daughters of thy brethren that thou goest to take a wife of the uncircumcised Philistines?" (Judg. 14:3). But Samson could only answer, "Get her for me, for she pleases me well." Sadness and sorrow descended upon his parents because they saw that this was the beginning of trouble for their wonderful son. The story is a sad experience. It involved days of weeping for Samson's wife, days of disappointment for him, and ultimately death for the entire family of the unfortunate girl who was involved in this episode (Judg. 14:5-15:6).

The next woman with whom Samson was involved was another Philistine in the capital of their country, Gaza. She was a common sinner of the city, and Samson became enamored with her. We can make no excuse for a man of God being guilty of an action like this, and the Scripture makes no excuse for him either. Samson had again succumbed to his own weakness. It is true that in the midst of the night his conscience warned him and he rose up in time to save his life, delivering himself by a mighty exploit of strength, but his downward path had begun. One cannot take fire into his bosom and not be burned. God had mercy upon Samson at this time, but it was of no avail (Judg. 16:1-3).

The third woman with whom Samson became involved was Delilah, another daughter of the Philistines, who had her home in the beautiful Valley of Sorek. In those days, Palestine's hills were covered with trees, and her valleys had streams of water, and thousands of people inhabited the land. Timnath and Sorek and Gaza were all near together in the south country of the Philistines. Here, beside a quiet river, Delilah had a garden and a home where she entertained her callers. Broken homes are due to women such as this. Our cities in America are full of them. It is because of them that divorces occur in one out of every four marriages. One wonders what a man expects to have when he exchanges a wife and a home for a woman such as this. A careful look at Samson ought to be a strong warning to any who are beset by such a sin. Samson's fall had begun with lust. First, the lust of the eyes, and then the lust of the flesh. Then he proceeded to lying, and finally to abandoning his Nazarite vow and his contract with God. Samson had ample warning against taking up with another Philistine woman after his experiences with the daughter of Timnath and with the woman of Gaza; and the fact that he went on is not only a reproach upon a judge of Israel but is a sad commentary upon the weakness of the man. Thus we behold him as one placed in a high position, elevated to the pinnacle of glory for those times, and yet destined to a most disgraceful fall because he sinned against the Spirit of God.

II. Delilah, the Woman Who Ruined Him

Anyone passing along the Valley of Sorek toward Eshtaol would have seen this beautiful little home with its vineyard and olive trees supported by the money of illicit love. It was inhabited by a famous but beautiful woman named Delilah. Probably this was not her true name but one assumed for her profession. Some think that Samson was married to this woman, but the Scripture gives no implication of this. She was merely the woman of Samson's choice in the hour of his weakness. The woman a man chooses reveals what he is. Delilah was physically beautiful but wanton. She misused her feminine appeal to an unusually disgraceful extent, but every woman who feigns love and indulges vanity and coquetry in order to obtain selfish ends is essentially like Delilah. Feminine charm is the gift of God. A woman has received it from her Creator. The appeal of love is that within the power of a woman, and God will certainly hold woman responsible for trifling with and misusing the fairest and best gift.

Delilah was brilliant and entertaining. Few men are infatuated over a long period of time only with beauty. One can hardly think that the fifty-year-old Julius Caesar would have become enamored and held over a long period of time by the twenty-one-year-old Cleopatra had she not been of a brilliant and entertaining nature as well as beautiful. Samson was irresistibly drawn to Delilah and returned to visit her often because she dazzled him with her wit and her brilliance. Delilah was unbelieving and hence was representative of heathen women. Heathenism knew nothing of the home life that Christianity has created. Woman was either a slave or she was a plaything of man. She was never considered his equal and never entered into the public life of a man. For their banquets and their public affairs, the heathen of antiquity depended upon a class of women such as Delilah. That Samson should have known better is very evident, but so should thousands of other men and women who even marry outside of their own religion. You simply cannot mix Christianity and unbelief, but it is impossible to tell young people this. They invariably come back in tears and heartache and disappointment because of the misunderstandings and the sorrows that arise therefrom. The Scripture says, "Be not unequally yoked together with unbelievers. What concord hath Christ with Belial?" (II Cor. 6:14, 15). It is no better to marry outside of the Christian faith today than it was to marry an unbeliever in the days of Samson. The person Samson chose was anything but a helpmate for a holy man of God.

From the narrative we may quickly sketch the character

of Delilah. First, she was selfish. It is clear from her dealings with the Philistines that she was covetous of money and wealth. She was ambitious, and she used Samson only to gain materially. Being proud of her ability as a lovemaker, she gloried in the fact that she was able to conquer the affections of the great Israelitish judge.

Second, she was false to the core. One might argue that she acted in behalf of her own country in order to deliver it from a great enemy and was only like unto Jael, who delivered the Israelites from Sisera, but the difference is that Jael never sold her husband or her lover for a price. Among women, Delilah takes her place as Judas does among men as a great traitor who sold a friend for a bribe.

Third, Delilah used her love for ulterior purposes. From the love Samson carried for her she could have responded and been true, but she only feigned love. In Delilah we have a woman with no principle, who was evil in every way we approach her character.

The influence of Delilah over Samson became stronger with every contact between the two. Samson's fall and ruin began in his first visit. The Scripture says, "There is a way which seemeth right unto a man, but the end thereof is death" (Prov. 14:12). Samson beheld these same practices on every hand round about him, yet he succumbed and became enslaved by this witch. He exchanged the glories of being judge of Israel and a servant of God, a Nazarite, for being the temporarily satisfied companion of a wanton woman. The influence of Delilah was entirely evil. It is true that a woman may lead a man either to heaven or to hell.

Delilah became the instrument of the Philistine lords. They, too, knew the weakness of Samson's nature, and so they offered her eleven hundred pieces of silver if she would deliver him into their hands. Delilah consented, and the result was a struggle of wit and love. One day Delilah said, "Tell me where your great strength lieth, Samson, and why is it that no one can bind you in order to overcome you at any time? You have done such wonderful things. What is the secret of it all?"

This should have revealed to Samson the desire of Delilah but, being so infatuated, he could not see through her craft. Jokingly, he replied that if they would bind him with seven green withes that were never dried, then he should be weak as any other man. While Samson slept, she so bound him and informed the Philistines to wait outside her chamber. Then she cried, "The Philistines be upon thee, Samson," and he rose up and broke the bonds as if they were a thread touched by the fire. He had mocked her, and inwardly she was very impatient and angry, but subtly she only reproached him for his lack of love, finally protesting that if he really loved her he ought not to keep any secrets from his dear Delilah.

After her third failure, she said, "How canst thou say, 'I love thee' when thine heart is not with me? Thou hast mocked me these three times and hast not told me wherein thy great strength lies." It must have seemed to him that his sin became less sinful in that he had given himself to a woman who in spite of her illicit practices had such an ideally beautiful conception of love. She pressed him day by day, and his soul was vexed unto death until he told her all his heart, namely, that the source of his strength was his Nazarite vow, that if his hair were shaved from him he would be as weak as any other man. This time Delilah saw that he had told her all his heart, so she summoned the Philistines and had them ready for the final assault. Samson should have been warned as to the nature of a Philistine woman by the seven days' weeping of the daughter of Timnath, which won from him his former secret of the riddle, but instead he allowed himself to be deceived and by a self-revelation of the secret of his power he broke his compact with God. She had attained her purpose.

III. The Ruin That Finally Engulfed Samson

Delilah caused Samson to sleep across her lap, and she called for a Philistine to come and shave off his hair. How the man must have trembled as he performed his task delicately and gently so as not to awake the giant! Once finished, she cried, "Samson, the Philistines be upon thee." He awoke out of his sleep and said as at other times, "I will go out and shake myself," and he wist not that the Lord had departed from him (Judg. 16:20). This is one of the saddest verses in the Bible. It depicts the state of a man who has known God and who has lost Him. It is the tragic state of being shelved in God's service. Concerning this, Paul said, "I keep under my body, and bring it into subjection; lest that by any means, when I have preached to others, I myself should be a castaway" (I Cor. 9:27). What he meant was that God should shelve him in his effective service. It is tragic, once having known the Spirit of the Lord, to have grieved Him away. Paul wrote, "Grieve not the Spirit of God whereby we are sealed against the day of redemption" (Eph. 4:30). Any besetting sin, any disobedience, any wickedness or evil in the life of the believer may cause him to grieve the Spirit of the Lord and thus to lose the victory.

Samson had been the great strong man, the unconquerable one, the overcomer, but once he had grieved the Spirit of the Lord away, he lost his victory. Without the Spirit of the Lord, the source of his strength, his power, his victory, and his exploits was gone. It was not Samson's hair that was the source of his strength: it was the fact that the hair was the symbol of the covenant between him and God; and when he broke the covenant by sin, God removed the Spirit of victory and power. It is all too common to see some spiritual giant of God, who has for ten, twenty, or forty years preached the Gospel of Christ with tremendous power and victory, ultimately stripped of the source of his power. On numerous occasions we have listened to men who have boasted of their past deeds but who today are doing absolutely nothing for their Lord. This is a tragic situation.

Samson went out and shook himself and thought he would defend himself from the Philistines, but he found that his strength had gone and they were able to afflict him and conquer him. Delilah had done what a battalion of Philistine soldiers had failed to do. How she must have gloried in the power of her attraction and in the fame she received therefrom! Samson's was a rude awakening. He did not know that the Spirit of God had departed from him. What an awakening comes to a person, a child of God, who through sin has lost the blessing of the Lord and as a result finds that he can no longer overcome the innumerable difficulties that beset him round about. The Philistines expressed their hatred and spite on him in gouging out his eyes, in binding him, and in afflicting him. They had discerned his weakness, and they had defeated him by it. Be sure that Satan knows exactly where your besetting sin lies and where your weakest point is, and he will strike you there again and again through temptation until you either defeat him once and for all or he brings you low.

The next scene in Samson's life is in the prison in Gaza. This prison is in the bottom of the house of Dagon, a god of the Philistines. There, in deep humiliation, Samson labors as a slave along with the other slaves, grinding at the mill. He is bound in fetters of brass and has only enough liberty to perform his task. Visitors pass by and laugh, jeer, and call out upon him asking, "Where is your strength now? Where is the God of Israel? Why do you not do some exploit now?" Samson's only reply is to grind more fiercely. There is a legend that Milton has incorporated in his great poem called "Samson Agonistes," in which Delilah is supposed to have come to visit Samson in his prison-house in order to implore his forgiveness for her base deed. He cries out:

> Out! Out! hyena, these are thy wonted arts,
> And arts of every woman false like thee;
> To break all faith, all vows, deceive, betray.
> Then as repentant, to submit, beseech,
> And reconcilement move with feign'd remorse.

Then Delilah urges her weakness, saying: "Nor shouldst thou have trusted that to woman's frailty." Then she adds, "Ere I to thee, thou to thyself was cruel." To which Samson replies, "How cunningly the sorceress displays her own transgressions to upbraid me mine!"

Delilah's statement was true. Before any woman can betray him or be cruel to him, man must betray and be cruel to himself. Yet Samson now made a final renunciation of her and turned his heart back to God. We know this because it says, "The hair of his head began to grow again after he was shaven." The entire implication is that Samson in the prison-house remembered the heights from which he fell, remembered his fellowship with God, and remembered that the source of his power and strength was in the Lord, and so turned unto Him.

The story ends with a bright spot in the life of Samson. He had grievously sinned, and that sin laid him low. His besetting sin had found him out, and he was defeated by it. As he was in the depths, during a great assembly of the Philistines, he was brought out to make sport, and before them he danced, broke beams, and demonstrated what strength he had, until weary. He asked the lad who led him to take him to the pillars of the house that he might rest. In that vast chamber there were some three thousand Philistines mocking him and praising their god for delivering him into their hands. Then Samson called upon the Lord and said, "O Lord God, remember me, I pray Thee, and strengthen me, I pray Thee, only this once, O God, that I may be at once avenged of the Philistines for my two eyes." Here he recognized that God was the source of his strength and of his blessing, and he turned unto Him. Samson had lost the presence of God, but he was not himself lost. His punishment was temporal, but the eternal guilt of his sin was remitted. A final gift of strength was given to him in answer to his prayer. He bowed himself, pulled on the pillars, and died in the mighty crash that followed. Here stands a man in whose life sin abounded, but grace did much more abound. By one act of repentance, he returned unto the Lord and was forgiven. So may you.

7

Ruth

The Woman Who Won a Husband

> And now, my daughter, fear not. I will do to thee all that
> thou requirest, for all the city of my people doth know that
> thou art a virtuous woman (Ruth 3:11).

This pastoral idyl begins with the statement, "When the
judges ruled Israel." The period of the Judges recalls the
storm and stress of Israel's history. It is hardly possible to
imagine that this beautiful pastoral scene should have taken
place in the period described in the Book of Judges. Here we
see a quiet scene of family life, of bereavement, of migration,
of poverty and of blessing, which has been designated as one
of the most excellent in literature, and in no way suggests the
wild, stormy period of the Judges. Here, in this story of Ruth,
is beauty, love, and truth exquisitely presented.

In this story, we have all the lights and the shadows of
human life presented. When Naomi returned from Moab, she
said to her companions in Bethlehem, "Call me not Naomi.
Call me Mara, for the Lord hath dealt very bitterly with me"
(Ruth 1:20). Naomi means "blessedness." Mara means "bitterness." These are the two aspects of human life, and they
are found in the Book of Ruth, for it begins with sorrow and
it ends with happiness. Thus it is that satisfaction and discon-
tent, hope and disappointment, achievement and failure, joy
and sorrow, follow every man and every woman through life.

It is said that this story of the heartaches and the joys of
a humble family can hardly be placed in the time of the

Judges, yet how little one would think if he read the headlines of the papers of our day that quiet church, family, and business life continue anywhere. The Book of Judges concerns itself with the headlines of four hundred and fifty years of history of Israel, whereas the Book of Ruth concerns itself with one generation. It is the contrast of flying over a great series of mountain ranges by airplane and of living in a quiet, green valley. In the valley, life moves slowly with the lowing of the herd and the bleating of the sheep, the growing of the oaks and the flowing of the river. Flying through the sky, life moves over great sections as the valleys pass under one's view. So it is in the Bible. It deals with the history of nations and cosmic movements, but it also occupies its attention with the life of human beings as such. It is an error for us to occupy our attention with either exclusively.

The events of the period of Judges are equal in length to the history of America from its earliest times to the present. Think of trying to encompass the history of the great leaders of America for this long period of time in a few pages so as to designate the general tenor of American life. Like in the Book of Judges, hideous sins of murder, war, civil struggle, oppression, and depression would follow each other successively. In Judges we read of Gideon, Jephthah, Barak, Samson, Shamgar, Ehud, and other mighty men who performed great deeds. We read of hideous scenes of immorality, of pillage, of murder, of oppression, and of wickedness. We read of periods of rising in spiritual life and again of falling on the part of the people, periods of prosperity and periods of depression, but the one clause that describes it all is that "every man did what was right in his own eyes" (Judg. 21:25). That standard is quite comparable to that of our own day, an individualistic one in which men have rejected any external standard of righteousness and do what is right in their own eyes. In this stormy, wild period was the simple, beautiful story before us now.

The narrative opens with an economic depression in which a seemingly good family was caught, much to its sorrow. There are certain cosmic movements in the world in which the righteous suffer with the wicked, in which it is not always a man's fault when he is down and out. Because a man suffers, one should not judge him as a greater sinner than someone else, for in these national or cosmic movements the rain falls upon the righteous and upon the wicked indiscriminately. Because of this depression, which had resulted from a famine in the land, the family of Elimelech, which included his wife Naomi and his two sons Mahlon and Chilion, departed from the land of Judah to go to Moab. Either Elimelech was discouraged with the conditions that existed under the judges or else out of unbelief he left his inheritance, to miss the chastisement of the Lord by going into another land, especially a land that was under the condemnation of the Lord.

Hence our story opens in the land of Moab. We want you to know how Ruth won a husband. And we want you to know the typical meaning of Ruth.

I. THE STORY OF RUTH

No sooner had the little family arrived in Moab than Elimelech, the father, took sick and died. It was a hard blow that struck Naomi, but its strength was lessened by the fact that she had two stalwart, faithful sons by her side. Happiness, which seemed so fleeting and elusive to this little family, now appeared to return again for a brief time, for the two sons found for themselves wives of the women of Moab. Chilion married a woman named Orpah, and Mahlon married Ruth. The unified household dwelt together for ten years, and then misfortune visited again, for the angel of death was hovering around the once desolate home, and this time summoned both Mahlon and Chilion. Poor Naomi now lost the last prop upon which she had leaned. The light of prosperity was gone, and gloom enveloped the sorrowing old woman.

Then, as happens so often in the lives of those of advanced years, she began to think of her old home, of her people and of her nation. She heard that the Lord had visited His people and had given them bread, and following her thoughts she turned her face toward Judea. Stating her determination to her daughters, she urged them both to tarry in Moab, where they might find rest with their own people and in their fathers' houses. Orpah accepted the advice and departed, but Ruth remained with Naomi and determined to return with her to Judea. One can well imagine what a change must have occurred in the little town during the time that Naomi was gone. The houses perhaps were the same and streets were the same, but many of her old companions were now gone. The famine had taken its toll, and the community cemetery had many new markers. Yet there were enough old friends there to greet her and to recognize the great difference in her. Instead of being in the bloom of womanhood, she now was old, bent, gray, wrinkled, and sorrowful, so that they even said, "Can this be Naomi?" Acknowledging that she was the same, she asked them to call her Mara, which means bitterness, because of her sorrow.

But Naomi was not alone, for Ruth had determined to go with her, and she became the only comfort Naomi had in her return. Together these two lovely women, who were very fond of one another, determined to face their trials bravely and in mutual forbearance. Hence, there is no implication of any complaint made one to another, nor is there ever any chiding or any spirit of strife. If love exists between women, it is a beautiful thing, because it is one of the highest of all forms of love. Here was one, not of mother and daughter, but of mother-in-law and daughter-in-law, which transcends even the best of blood relationship. Ruth urged her mother-in-law to allow her to go to work as a gleaner in the harvest, and finally Naomi acceded to the request and allowed her to go. Through her work, Ruth became acquainted with the owner of the field in which she happened to be gleaning. After many kindnesses, which manifested the concern and the heart interest of the owner of the field, Boaz, for Ruth, Ruth appealed to him as a kinsman redeemer to marry her. To this Boaz responded. The marriage was performed in the gate of the city of Bethlehem. Ruth and Naomi were taken to his home, and before long a little life made its advent into the world, their son Obed, so that the women of Bethlehem sang and praised Naomi, saying that her daughter-in-law, Ruth, had been better to her than seven sons and that the Lord through her had restored Naomi's life and nourished her old age.

As one reads and rereads this story, the outstanding characteristic of it is the recognition of the Lord. The Lord is given the central place by all characters in the narrative. First Naomi, being most prominent, draws our attention. She is the one who suffered most, and yet everything that came to her in the lights and shadows of her life was of the Lord. When loss after loss struck the little home in Moab until Naomi was left desolate of her husband and her two sons, she confessed to her daughter-in-law that all of this had been of the Lord. In her solemn plea to both of them to turn back to their fathers' houses because of the darkness and gloom of the outlook, she said, "For it grieveth me much for your sakes that the hand of the Lord is gone out against me" (Ruth 1:13). Later when Naomi returned to Bethlehem, she said to her friends and companions, "The Almighty hath dealt very bitterly with me. I went out full and the Lord hath brought me home again empty," and "Why then call ye me Naomi seeing the Lord hath testified against me and the Almighty hath afflicted me?" Evidently Naomi here confessed that she had been the moving spirit in the migration of the family from Bethlehem to Moab, and she recognized that everything was of the Lord. It is even written that she acknowledged that the end of the famine in Bethlehem was due to the Lord, for she said that the Lord had visited His people in giving them bread (Ruth 1:6). This reinforces the belief that it was because of an act of unbelief on the part of Naomi that the little family went to Moab. And, finally, in Naomi's life, we have the recognition that their good fortune and their restoration and their blessing were of the Lord.

Similarly, Ruth placed the Lord central in the whole of her life. She had been born and brought up in a country where the god Chemosh was worshiped, to whom human sacrifices were given and under whose worship the nation had degen-rated into a group of licentious people indulging every physical whim, but when she learned of the Lord, she rejected Chemosh, the idol, and chose the Lord as her God. This decision we shall examine a little later, and it was of great religious value, a true conversion of Ruth. Later we find that the narrative says, "It was her hap to light upon the field of Boaz" (Ruth 2:3). Here is definite implication of the place of Providence in Ruth's life. Many are the fortuitous occurrences in the lives of us all, which begin a chain of events leading to some great crisis in our lives. God plays a part in the smallest things of our lives. Ruth also obeyed Naomi in the Lord. She recognized that she was now serving Naomi's God, and in the smallest things she followed the desires of her mother Naomi.

Likewise Boaz put the Lord first in his life. When he came from Bethlehem to his reapers, he said to them in greeting, "The Lord be with you." They answered him, "The Lord bless thee" (Ruth 2:4). Whether it was the famine or religion that had taught them, these men recognized that their prosperity was of the Lord. Likewise, when Boaz discovered Ruth working in his field and had addressed her, he said, "The Lord recompense thy work and a full reward be given thee of the Lord God of Israel under Whose wings thou art come to trust" (Ruth 2:12). Boaz recognized Ruth's choice of coming to Judah as a religious choice of the Lord as her God, and he believed that the Lord would recompense her. Moreover, when Ruth ultimately settled upon him as the kinsman redeemer rather than some younger man, he said to her, "Blessed be thou of the Lord, my daughter, for thou hast showed more kindness in the latter end than at the beginning" (Ruth 3:10). Everything for Boaz was either of the Lord or for the Lord.

Similarly, even the people placed the Lord central in their thought and in their speech. When Boaz brought this girl to the gates of the city in order that he might take her as his wife before the people, they cried, "The Lord make the woman that is come into thy house like Rachel and Leah, which two did build the house of Israel" (Ruth 4:11). Only under the Lord could Boaz in the eyes of the people have the blessing upon his own house through this woman. Finally, when Obed was born, the people said unto Naomi, "Blessed be the Lord which hath not left thee this day without a kinsman that His name may be famous in Israel" (Ruth 4:14). It was God who had heard Naomi's prayer, and it was God who had sent the kinsman redeemer to her. Thus even the story itself is centered upon the Lord, for the descendant of Obed was none other than David, who was to be the progenitor of Christ, for David said, "The Lord said to my lord, sit thou upon my right hand until I make thy foes thy footstool" (Ps. 110:1). Everything in the story of Ruth centers about the Lord.

Ruth had a beautiful conversion to the Lord. I suppose that in a nominal way she had embraced the Lord as the object of her worship during the time when Naomi's two sons were still living. Here is a case of the faith of the husband sanctifying the wife and leading her into the true religion, but the day came when that sympathy toward the religion of her husband had to become a reality, for she was faced with a choice between two kinds of life. Moab offered her security, rest, and perhaps a new husband through her own people and her father's house. In Israel she had nothing to look forward to but strangeness, possible poverty, the burden of supporting the aged Naomi, work by her hands, and loneliness from all of her friends and her people. It was no small decision on the part of Ruth to follow the still, small voice that led her on in the pathway of duty, of love, and of faith instead of following the way Orpah took of personal satisfaction and ease.

We are not to think that the influence of Naomi was slight in this matter. It is a great truth that the personal influence of believers does more to lead men to Christ than their words. Naomi had passed through a harrowing time of sorrow and trial, but even in the midst of all she demonstrated the validity of her faith in God, and this faith and this God commended themselves to Ruth. Ruth not only had conceived a mighty love for her mother-in-law, which was able to make her willing to support her in her old age, but she made a choice of Naomi's God. As the three of them stood out on the west of Moab's hills before they descended into the Jordan Valley that should ultimately lead over into Judah, Naomi said, "Go, return each to her mother's house: the Lord deal kindly with you, as ye have dealt with the dead, and with me. The Lord grant you that ye may find rest, each of you in the house of her husband" (Ruth 1:8, 9). Then Naomi kissed them, and they all wept. It was a sad hour. Both of the girls rose to the occasion and said, "Surely we will return with thee unto thy people." But again Naomi told them to turn again and to go to their fathers' houses. Orpah kissed her mother-in-law and left. For the third time, Naomi addressed Ruth and said, "Behold, thy sister-in-law is gone back unto her people and unto her gods: return thou after thy sister-in-law." The emphasis here upon gods of Moab and the God of the Israelites reveals that this was a distinctly religious decision. Ruth then uttered the words for which she has become immortal: "Entreat me not to leave thee or to return from following after thee: for whither thou goest, I will go; and where thou lodgest I will lodge; thy people shall be my people, and thy God my God: where thou diest, will I die, and there will I be buried: the Lord do so to me, and more also, if aught but death part thee and me" (Ruth 1:16, 17).

Hereafter the Lord was to be Ruth's God. She had passed her crisis. She had turned unto the Lord. She was truly converted. She had made the decision and was lifted into a place where a divine kinsman redeemer would be available for her.

II. How Ruth Won a Husband

Ruth was not distinguished for her beauty, but for her character. Others such as Eve, Sarah, Rebekah, and Rachel were famed because the Bible says they were fair to look upon, but never once is this said concerning Ruth. It may well be that Ruth was a comely person, but there is no hint of beauty concerning her in the Bible. We cannot even think that Ruth was young. She had been married for ten years to Mahlon and now was a widow. Yet when Boaz saw her gleaning after his reapers in the field, his eye, which was accustomed to the flotsam and jetsam of Bethlehem and Judea, was able to pick her out among the gleaners in his field. Something about her bearing, her modesty, her demeanor, was different from that of the other women. He was led to ask the chief of his reapers, "Whose damsel is this?" And then it was that he heard the story of all that Ruth had done for Naomi, because of her belief in Naomi's God.

The ancient Israelites, under the law of God, had a very beautiful custom of allowing a provision to be made for the poor. It was contrary to divine law for men to reap the corners of their field or to beat their fruit-trees twice or to gather up the materials that had fallen from the reapers. This must be left for the poor. Hence, the poor followed the reaper in the fields, gleaning and gathering up what they could. They also plucked the fruit that was not ripe at the time of the first beating of the trees, and they took their little produce from the corners of the field left unreaped. It was in this activity that Ruth was now engaged when she fell under the interest of Boaz. It should be remembered that by law, when a man died leaving a widow and no children to carry on his name in the tribe, his nearest kinsman was required to marry his widow, and the first-born child of the new marriage was to take the name of the dead man in order that no family should perish out of the tribes of Israel. This was called the law of a kinsman redeemer. Boaz was a near kinsman to Naomi and hence was also a near kinsman to Ruth, and according to the law it was her right to demand this privilege from Boaz.

But Boaz demonstrated his heart interest in Ruth long before she ever made any claim to his part as a kinsman redeemer. He told her that she could freely reap after the young men, that they would not bother her though it was a rather violent period when a woman's virtue was not of much value, and that she could drink of the water the young men had drawn. He also invited her to come and eat at his table during the season of rest. Then he commanded the young men to allow some handfuls to fall on purpose for her. When Ruth asked him, "Why have I found grace in thine eyes that thou shouldest take knowledge of me, seeing I am a stranger?" Boaz replied, "It has been fully shown me all that thou hast done unto thy mother-in-law since the death of thine husband." Boaz' interest in Ruth had been due to her character. She had a fine reputation. Later he said to her, "All the city of my people know that thou art a virtuous woman." They knew that she was a woman who had chosen the Lord. She had become a convert to Israel's God. They knew that with great care she had taken an interest in the aged Naomi, willing to work to keep her in food. They knew that she had sacrificed every comfort of life in order to return to this land with her mother-in-law. She had left her father and her mother and the land of her nativity and had come to a strange people.

Boaz also learned that she was a willing worker. His chief of the reapers said, "She has continued among the gleaners even from morning until now except that she tarried a little in the house" (Ruth 2:7). From early morning until nearly noon, Ruth worked with only a little rest, and that trip to the house was probably due to the fact that she was unaccustomed to the difficult work of gleaning in the field. Here was a woman who was not too proud to work, and when she did not have much, she was willing to take less in order that she might keep alive.

Boaz learned that she was an obedient daughter, for her actions in some cases could only have been instigated by Naomi, and thus she was only performing Naomi's will. No wonder that the women said of Ruth, "She is better to thee than seven sons" (Ruth 4:15). She was fulfilling one of the original commandments.

The outcome of the matter was very happy. At the instigation of Naomi, Ruth ultimately made her claim on Boaz for a kinsman redeemer. She said, "Spread thy skirt over thy daughter, for thou art a near kinsman to me" (Ruth 3:9). This was a plea for marriage. The circumstances of the event reveal that Boaz' affection had already been claimed by the woman, and he was more than willing to perform the duty. He, in turn, demonstrated his wisdom and his care in order that his own name should be irreproachable and that Ruth might soon find rest. In accordance with the custom of the day, he went immediately following the harvest to the gate of the city where the elders of the people must pass by. There this righteous and just man sought out his own relative who was a nearer kinsman to Ruth than himself and asked him if he would do the kinsman duty to Ruth, for he had the privilege first of all of purchasing Mahlon's land and of raising up a posterity to Mahlon's name. This kinsman refused the duty because it would mar his own inheritance and asked Boaz to take the responsibility upon himself (Ruth 4:6). Then it was that Boaz declared his intention to buy all of Elimelech's and Chilion's and Mahlon's land out of the hand of Naomi, which would make her a wealthy woman, and to take Ruth the Moabitess to be his wife and to raise up the name of the dead upon his inheritance. This generous act was applauded by the people, who in turn became witness to the marriage there in the gate and invoked the divine blessing upon them, that they might become as Rachel and Leah were to Jacob, building the house of Israel. The results of this union were that a son was born to whom Naomi became the nurse and Ruth the mother, a son which in turn was the progenitor of Christ, who was the Saviour of Ruth's own soul through her decision.

III. The Typical Meaning of Ruth

I suppose we could stop the story here, but we cannot without mentioning the remarkable typology contained in this book. There is a typical meaning to all of the characters that ought to be recognized, because it bears a vital truth for the individual Christian.

Naomi undoubtedly is typical of Israel, who in unbelief was dispersed among the heathen, passing through trial and sorrow and suffering, but ultimately recognizing that the chastisement was of the Lord and thereby repenting and returning to the land of Israel, accompanied by a believing and redeemed church, called out from among the heathen that both might be blessed through a kinsman Redeemer. The place of Israel today is the place of Naomi in Moab under chastisement,

under fire and suffering and trial. When will the Israelites see
that they went out full but the Lord has brought them back
empty? When will they turn in repentance unto the Lord?
It is their only hope. There were the Moabite women, Orpah
and Ruth. Moab was a degenerate people, the individuals of
whom were not allowed to stand in the congregation of the
Lord to the tenth generation. God's judgment was upon them.
They represent the heathen world — the Gentiles — and Orpah
is typical of the unbelieving heathen who have had an opportunity to accept the knowledge of the true God and who continue in unbelief. Ruth, however, represents the Gentile church
called out of heathenism, responding to the message of the
true God and opening her heart unto the gospel of grace. In
Ruth we see a picture of the church as the New Testament
describes it, redeemed and prepared to be the bride of the
Redeemer.

Boaz represents the Redeemer, the Lord Jesus Christ,
the mighty man of spiritual wealth, the one who can raise
up the name of the dead upon his inheritance. He is the one
for whom God has prepared the church, and He will be
married to the church in mystical union, thus becoming a
kinsman Redeemer to it and the restorer of Israel's life, for
when Christ is married to the church, Israel will be restored
to spiritual life. Israel is now in blindness and in unbelief,
but when Christ and the church are married, Israel will receive benefit. All that Boaz did for Ruth is typical of what
Christ has done for the church.

The events of the wedding in the gate in the midst of
all of the people is typical of the great wedding feast of the
Lamb. The great Book of Ephesians says that "Christ also
loved the church and gave Himself for it that He might
sanctify and cleanse it with the washing of water by the
Word, that He might present it to Himself a glorious church,
not having spot or wrinkle or any such thing, but that it
should be holy and without blemish . . . this is a great mystery, but I speak concerning Christ and the church."

It was for this purpose that Christ died for the church that

He might make it perfect in holiness and ultimately take it unto Himself. The Bible also says that this marriage feast of the Lamb is to be held in the heavenlies, for the day is coming when the heavens will open and the Lamb of God will return to receive His bride and take her away to the great wedding feast. The Bible describes this as saying, "And I heard as it were a great voice of a multitude and as the voice of many waters and of the voice of mighty thunderings, saying, Hallelujah, for the Lord God omnipotent reigneth. Let us make glad and rejoice and give honor to Him for the marriage of the Lamb is come and His wife hath made herself ready. And to her was granted that she should be arrayed in fine linen, clean and white, for the fine linen is the righteousness of the saints. And he saith unto me, Write, blessed are they which are called unto the marriage supper of the Lamb." Happy is the man who will have part in that great wedding supper of the Lamb. The entire Book of Ephesians was written to define the destiny of the church. The church is to be the peculiar and particular inheritance of the Lord Jesus Christ. It is to share His glory in the ages to come.

What a privilege, then, to participate in membership in the church of the living God! This depends upon being saved and purified now through the blood of the Lamb. In the company of the redeemed are various groups, such as an innumerable company of angels, the general assembly and church of the firstborn, and the spirits of just men made perfect. The only way to become a member of the church is to be born again. "Except a man be born again he cannot see the kingdom of God." Every born-again person is a member of the church of Jesus Christ and part of His bride to participate in the glories that are to come. He also may live today under the protection of the kinsman Redeemer. Every person stands either in the relationship of Orpah or of Ruth or of Naomi to Christ. If you are a Jew in unbelief, you are as Naomi was in the Land of Moab. If you are an unbeliever, a Gentile, you are as Orpah, who was rejecting the light. If you are a believer, you are as Ruth, or one who has been converted to the kinsman Redeemer.

Perhaps you have never made your decision, and now is the hour for you to choose your Redeemer. Remember the words of Ruth, "Thy God shall be my God. Thy people shall be my people. Where thou dwellest I will dwell." Can you say that? Is the God of the Christians your God? Are the Christians your people? Are you dwelling in the heavenly places now? Have you chosen the Lord? Are you willing to leave all for a kinsman Redeemer Who will break your bonds of sin and servitude and lift you to freedom and rest in the kingdom of God? Do you know what it means to have mystical union with Christ now and the promise of full union hereafter as His bride to share with Him in ruling the universe? This is all your privilege and your opportunity, but it rests with you. Choose you. Will you have the world's greatest Lover? Will you be pure and spotless and worthy of being espoused? He will redeem you by His own precious blood now. You may then be presented to Him without spot or without wrinkle in holiness and love.

8

Hannah

The Woman Whose Prayer Was Answered

*And she vowed a vow, and said, O Lord, if thou wilt indeed
look on the affliction of thine handmaid, and wilt not forget
thine handmaid, but wilt give unto thine handmaid a man
child, then will I give him unto the Lord all the days of
his life* (I Sam. 1:11).

Hannah was a woman who became a mother by prayer
and faith. She is singled out and mentioned in Scripture because of her importance to God as a mother in Israel. Hers is
a most human story of life.

Hannah had all the environmental causes for basic insecurity according to modern psychology. She had division in
the home, she was misunderstood by her husband, she suffered
a lack of discernment by her priest and she endured the loss
of her child. Yet in spite of all this, she was a triumphant
believer.

Hannah was the first wife of Elkanah, a responsible and
righteous man in Israel, and had no children. Or else she
was a second wife taken when the mother of Elkanah's children was getting older. If she was a second wife, she had
violated the fundamental institution of marriage which, in the
creation ordinance, was monogamous, and hence she deserved
the trouble into which she got. The probabilities are, however,
that she was a first wife who was barren and who saw a rival
come into her home because of this barrenness, a practice
which was permitted by the Mosaic law. In any case, it was a

90

violation of the divine institution of marriage and wherever polygamy has been introduced it has brought nothing but sorrow. A study of the contention between Jacob's wives, the ill feeling between Abraham's wives, and similar situations of Scripture illustrate this. Anything which is contrary to God's revealed standard of marriage is wrong and is productive of evil. People may think that they can temporize with God's law, whether living in the day of Elkanah or living today, but they must suffer the consequence.

Envy entered this household and one wife provoked the other to fret and to bitterness. Wherever envying exists between women there is fretfulness and bitterness, whether in society, in the church, in business or in the home. The fruits of this sin of envy are often worse than many that are considered more heinous in the social register. For this reason, Alexander White had cards printed and circulated throughout his congregation which asked three questions: Is it true? Is it kind to repeat it? And, Is it necessary to repeat it? Observance of these rules would keep many of us from things which cause pain.

The favoritism which necessarily existed in Elkanah's household brought forth fruit in strife. Hannah was loved more than Peninnah and this was displayed by her receiving a larger portion when the gifts were distributed for presenting in the temple. Peninnah displayed her fine family, which made her superior, and through such a display mocked Hannah. Here was the same spirit that existed between Hagar and Sarah, the women of Abraham. Elkanah foolishly thought that he could take the place of a baby for a woman who wished to be a mother. Hence, the whole picture is one of division, of misunderstanding, of lack of discernment, of strife and bitterness. Woe unto those who find themselves in such a family situation. Hannah found her way of exit through prayer.

The Atmosphere of Prayer

Hannah was a woman who believed in God. God, for the family of Elkanah, was the source of all blessing. They wor-

shiped Him in the home and they worshiped Him in the temple. They sought to obey His law and they set God first in their lives. Even Hannah recognized a purpose in God's denying her desire. In spite of all this faith, they experienced their trouble in the home.

Back of this story is a most important truth which needs re-emphasis, namely, that the kind of men we have depends upon the mothers in a nation. A group of women were talking about when they should begin to train their children. One believed that it should be at the age of discretion, another one believed that it should be when the child began to talk, another believed it should be when the child was born. An old grandmother was listening and she observed, "Begin the training of your child twenty years before it is born." This emphasizes the importance of the mother. God was looking for a man to lead His people in the critical condition which existed at the end of the period of the judges. Israel was completely overlorded by the Philistines. Moral degeneracy had set in as is illustrated by the condition of Eli's sons (I Sam. 2:12, 17, 22). These children of the priest committed adultery, abhorred the sacrifice of the Lord and taught the people to abhor the sacrifice of the Lord. A change had to be inaugurated and in order to inaugurate it, God needed a man whom He could trust. He was literally looking here and there through Israel for such a man and He could find none. Therefore, He set about to prepare a mother.

He chose this woman Hannah, who was a woman of faith and prayer, and withheld her desire from her in order that through this discipline He might prepare her to be the mother of the man He desired. Childlessness among the Jewish women was a sign of reproach, a symbol of condemnation from God. Hannah's rival, Peninnah, used this as a source of provocation to her and mockery. She probably taught her children to be disrespectful to Hannah and many occasions arose within the home of tension, of provocation and of strife. Hannah resorted to prayer and yet her hope was deferred through the years as was the hope of the wife of Manoah, the hope of Rachel, the hope of Sarah and the hope of Elizabeth, all of whom were prevented from having a child by the divine purpose. Surely this Biblical fact should cause us to recognize that God desires to discipline mothers so that He can have children whom He can use. If ever the world needed such children and hence such mothers, it is now. The greatest thing a woman can do is to give a godly, trained, upright man to the world.

Hence, we note that Hannah's faith in God was part of her preparation for the birth of Samuel. We may contrast this with the materialistic conception of life which gives God no place, which has no recognition for grace, which has no interest in the church, and which never seeks to find wisdom and divine help. People who are materialists instead of being softened and made tender by the disappointments of life, as was Hannah, are hardened and embittered by them. When children come into such materialistic homes, they often create more problems than they solve. There is an army of orphaned children in the United States who have been made such by the divisions and strifes and separations in unbelieving homes. If one-third of the marriages of this nation end up in divorce or separation, we may be sure that these broken homes are the source of our delinquency, our immorality, disrespect and crime. A generation of hardened and embittered men and women who are materialists will not raise children who are obedient to God and desirous of exalting His name. There is a direct proportion between the breakup of the American homes and the abandonment of their faith in God. If Christ were the head of the households of America, our youth problems would not exist. We may trace the problem of delinquency back to liquor drinking, self-indulgent, selfish licentious parents who cannot give children of any value to society. In contrast with all this, Hannah was a woman who believed in God and prayed for God's highest gift, namely, a child.

Hannah believed that her solution was in prayer and as we can see from this Scripture, she practiced it. I believe in prayer. I have read many books which ascribe prayer to a psychological exercise which has only subjective affects upon the individual who prays, but my faith is established in the prayer promises of the Bible. In order to believe in prayer, we have to believe in the God of the Bible who is self-existent, other-worldly and independent, who created the world and who can interfere in the course of the world or use the laws of the world for His own purposes. We must believe that God in His omniscience foreknew our prayers and therefore set in motion those courses which would answer our prayers. We must believe that through prayer we are co-laborers with God and we set in motion spiritual forces. All this I believe. For 20 years I have kept a prayer list and on it I have literally hundreds of requests which have been marked off as answered. These have dealt with every phase of life from travel to the birth of children, to investment of money and time, to ministry and to every detail of human living. Happy is the individual who can ask God for the guidance and wisdom he needs in his ministry through prayer.

Hannah believed that God could and would answer her problem and give her a child. In fact, she was more specific. She wanted a son. She believed that God is the source of the life which is given to individuals. If you are a mother, remember that God gave you that child and you must answer to God for his life. When Hannah prayed in the tabernacle and asked God for a son and dedicated him back to God in the same breath, Eli finally discerned that she was a spiritual, pious, godly woman and he said, "The God of Israel grant thee thy petition." Then Hannah believed God, worshiped God, participated in the fellowship and returned to her home with no more sadness because she believed that God would solve her problem.

THE POWER OF PRAYER

We ought to study the nature of Hannah's prayers. First, these prayers were fervent. She prayed so fervently that her lips moved while the sound of her voice was silent, and while she swayed back and forth so that the aged Eli thought that she was under the influence of liquor. When the sacrifice of their family had been offered for their sins and they had eaten in fellowship with the priest, Hannah then rose and went into the tabernacle to pray. As Eli observed her in the bitterness of her soul, weeping and praying before the Lord, he thought that she was one of the women who lounged about the tabernacle with his sons, Hophni and Phinehas, and said, "How long wilt thou be drunken? Put away thy wine from thee." This very description reveals how intense and fervent was the prayer of Hannah. Her lips moved, her body swayed and she resembled a drunken woman. Have your prayers ever affected you in such a manner? James says, "The effectual fervent prayer of a righteous man availeth much" (James 5:16). This emphasis upon fervency is reinforced by the teaching of Jesus with all of His promises to those who ask, seek and knock and even the illustration of His commendation given to the Syro-Phoenician woman who continued to persist even though rebuked by Christ until she received her answer.

Too much of our praying is careless, cold, unmoved and unmoving and then we wonder why we do not receive answers. How do you pray? Do you merely kneel down before retiring and mumble a few things in your pillow before going to bed? Do you merely send forth ejaculatory prayers from time to time to the Lord? Or do you really have a time when you pray through on a prayer list and intelligently present your requests unto God? Unless you are moved by desire and your prayers are fervent, you will never move God.

Moreover, Hannah expressed her prayer. She did not speak audibly but she expressed it with her lips. Bishop Moule declared that it was very difficult for him to pray with concentration unless he gave some kind of expression to his prayer. I believe that is true. I think much of our praying is mere day-dreaming instead of fervent intercession. It is necessary for us to express our petition. Hannah was literally intriguing the Lord.

All this should be contrasted with Elkanah's praying. He undoubtedly prayed in the home and he went once a year to the tabernacle to offer his sacrifice and to pray there and he was probably a righteous, pious, God-fearing man, but he never wrestled in prayer for the answer to his wife's desire in spite of his being the patriarch and priest of the family. He was a good, sympathetic, loving man but a man of no great faith. This in itself may have held Hannah back in her high and divine purposes and yet she overcame the difficulty. The difference between Elkanah and Hannah is the difference between a passive believer and one who lays hold upon the promises of God in faith and in fervent prayer. Samuel stands as a monument to the fervency, sincerity and profundity of Hannah's prayers.

Hannah prayed the prayer of faith. She had, no doubt, read or heard read the five books of Moses and she knew of Moses' intercession with God on behalf of Israel and of the remarkable answers to prayer which he obtained. She acted upon such a precedent. We today have a Bible full of promises which are most remarkable and which cover the full extent of human living. If we would take these promises as a blank check from God and cash them in faith, claiming them, they would be ours. As long as they are merely objective and remain in the Bible unused and unappropriated, they will not be ours. Let us freely use these promises of God, remembering that whatsoever things we desire we are to believe that we have received them and we will have them (Mark 11:24).

The foundation of Hannah's prayer was her self-dedication. We note the nature of the prayer which she prayed (I Sam. 10:11). In this prayer she vowed unto the Lord that if He would answer her prayers and give her a man-child, that he would be dedicated unto the Lord all the days of his life. This meant that Hannah would have to return the child which God would give in dedication to God and lose him as soon as he was a young boy in order to have him serve the Lord. Her dedication is illustrated by her consecrating the answer to her prayers to God before she received that answer. This better than all things illustrates the dedication of Hannah. Hannah was now in the place where God could answer her prayer. For 20 or more years she had been disciplined through the failure to receive her desire, through unanswered prayer of deferred answers, until she came to the place of full consecration. If you have unanswered prayers, perhaps there is a reason. Perhaps God is withholding or deferring the answer to your prayer in order that He might deal with you to bring you to the place where He can trust you with the answer.

THE EFFECT OF PRAYER

Hannah believed the Lord and immediately ceased her grieving and fretting and departed from the tabernacle with joy and confidence for she believed the promise of Eli, the high priest, "her countenance was no more sad." In due season Samuel was conceived and then after the fulfillment of Hannah's time, was born. Those days must have been days of meditation upon the Word of God, of prayers of gratitude and thanksgiving, and of worship by Hannah. For when Hannah ultimately brought Samuel to the tabernacle to deliver him over to Eli as a minister and for him to begin the service of the Lord, she prayed a prayer which was weighted with Scripture and with profound implications of faith (I Sam. 2:1-10). All this was the fruit of her meditation during the days before Samuel was born. Then came the day when Samuel was born. What rejoicing to Elkanah, what satisfaction to Hannah and what a rebuke to Peninnah. Little did anyone know of the stature of this child who was born, of the ministry which he would perform in Israel and of the greatness of his prophetic office.

Hannah named the child Samuel, or "answer of God." Thus he was to carry the token throughout all his life that he had a peculiar relationship to God. A study of the names people bear will often reveal the interest and point of emphasis of the parents at the time of their birth. Once, in my evangelistic ministry, I tarried in a home where there were seven children and every child bore a Biblical name. This household was one of prayer, of Bible reading, of piety and of beautiful character, all of which revealed the faith of the parents expressed in the lives of those children.

In these early years Hannah coddled and nestled the child, prayed with him and for him, taught him what truths she knew, instructed him in the care of himself so that he could be independent, all in the light of the fact that she was to present him to the Lord in the temple. For some this might have been a shadow over one's early life but for her it was a source of joy for she knew he had been given by God and to God she would give him back. Those were days of intense pleasure in their home as Hannah enjoyed Samuel, trained him and looked forward to the day when she would dedicate him in that tabernacle.

She made up her mind that she would not return for the yearly sacrifice until Samuel was old enough to become a minister of Eli in the tabernacle.

When Samuel was a child with some degree of independence and self-sufficiency so that he could be of use to Eli, Hannah took a very liberal offering with her and brought the child to offer her thanksgiving in the house of the Lord and to leave the child with the aged Eli. She testified to him after her sacrifice. "Oh, my lord, as thy soul liveth, my lord, I am the woman that stood by thee here, praying unto the Lord. For this child I prayed; and the Lord hath given me my petition which I asked of him: therefore also I have lent him to the Lord; as long as he liveth." Thus Hannah and Samuel worshiped the Lord. Are we to believe that Hannah did not know of the conditions in Israel at that time? These conditions are marked by immorality in the temple (1 Sam. 2:22) and of transgression of the law of the Lord by the people, the fountain head of which was Eli's own sons. She could have argued with the Lord that to have brought this tender child into their association would corrupt him and turn him from the high purposes which she had in mind for him. Instead of that, she put her faith in God and His promise, left Samuel in the center of corruption believing that God would reveal Himself unto Samuel. Returning to her home, she must have been very lonely at first. But God accepted her sacrifice and made it up to Hannah so that she became the mother of several other children (I Sam. 2:21).

Hannah followed Samuel with her prayers. We read that year by year she brought a garment for him to wear. This was homespun but it was a garment made by hands of love and into it went the most precious wool from Elkanah's flock. Each time that Samuel put it on, every time he fingered that garment, he thought of his mother and her prayers and this became an anchor for him to protect him from the temptations and the examples of sin which he saw on every hand. Because Hannah had entrusted him to the Lord, in due season the Lord appeared unto Samuel and the word of the Lord was made known unto him. When Samuel came to serve Eli he did not yet know the Lord. He had been brought up in a godly environment, but he as yet did not have a personal religious experience. But here in the tabernacle God appeared to him, made His will known to him, and revealed His Word to him so that he was established to become a prophet of the Lord. In due season, Hannah must have died but we may well understand that the prophet Samuel, throughout his whole life, wore a garment like unto that which his mother had made and which ever reminded him of that pious, praying, believing woman of God.

Thus, Hannah participated in the deliverance of Israel and in the rule over Israel by God through His prophet for 40 years. She had a part in the establishment of the kingdom under David because Samuel had anointed David to become king before he died. Thus, Samuel was established before the Lord and before the people. Great was Hannah's contribution to Israel.

What place will your children take in the leadership of the church and nation? Will it be a result of your prayers and of your faith? What are you making of that child that God gave you? Are you a worthy parent at the pinnacle of success? Will he look back with gratitude to his home and to his family environment? This Samuel did because he made Ramah his home during his entire ministry (I Sam. 7:17; 25:1).

9

Abigail

THE WOMAN WHO COMBINED BEAUTY AND TACT

And David said to Abigail, Blessed be the Lord God of Israel which hath sent thee this day to meet me: and blessed be thy advice, and blessed be thou, which hast kept me this day from coming to shed blood (I Sam. 25:32,33).

Abigail is described as "a woman of good understanding, and of a beautiful countenance" (I Sam. 25:3). This is an unbeatable combination. Often beauty is combined with foolishness, or lightness, while wisdom proverbially is found in the homely, such Socrates or Lincoln. But for both beauty and wisdom to be combined in one person is an unusual circumstance.

Our attention is called to Abigail in the midst of the story of David's wanderings as an outlaw. David was anointed to be king of Israel when God rejected Saul because of his disobedience in regard to the Amalekites. God commanded Saul to exterminate this people because of the way in which they had harassed the Israelites in their journeys from Egypt to Canaan and had smitten or captured the stragglers of the people. The Amalekites had openly fought against Israel and had been defeated. They also were composed of a degenerate and corrupt people. It is difficult for us, in the light of the New Testament and of modern humanitarianism, to understand how God could command the destruction of a whole people. Nevertheless, this is the direct teaching of the Old Testament and we are to accept it at its face value. It is a revelation of an attribute of God which has been overlooked in modern theology and in modern Christian thinking.

Saul, instead of fulfilling God's commandment, spared the best of the sheep and of the oxen and the fatlings of the lambs in order that he might sacrifice them unto the Lord, and he destroyed everything which was vile and refuse. He also took alive Agag of the Amalekites. Because of this, Samuel, the judge of Israel, said, "Wherefore then didst thou not obey the voice of the Lord, but didst fly upon the spoil, and didst evil in the sight of the Lord? . . . Hath the Lord as great delight in burnt offerings and sacrifices, as in obeying the voice of the Lord? Behold, to obey is better than sacrifice, and to hearken than the fat of rams. For rebellion is as the sin of witchcraft, and stubborness is as iniquity and idolatry. Because thou hast rejected the word of the Lord, he hath also rejected thee from being king" (I Sam. 15:19, 22, 23). After this, Samuel came no more to see Saul until the day of his death, but he mourned for Saul.

Then it was that the Lord sent Samuel to anoint David, the son of Jesse, the Bethlehemite whom he had chosen to be king. As Jesse caused his sons to pass before Samuel, God said unto Samuel, "Look not on his countenance, or on the height of his stature; because I have refused him: for the Lord seeth not as man seeth; for man looketh on the outward appearance, but the Lord looketh on the heart" (I Sam. 16:7). After seven of Jesse's sons had passed by and had been rejected, Samuel said, "Are here all thy children?" And Jesse said, "There remaineth yet the youngest, and, behold, he keepeth the sheep." Samuel commanded that he be sent for and when he came he was of a beautiful countenance and goodly to look upon, so Samuel arose and anointed him to be king of Israel. From that day, the Spirit of the Lord came upon David and the Spirit of the Lord departed from Saul.

Henceforth, David was marked to be king. In the providential circumstances, he was chosen to be the harpist at Saul's court where he soothed the spirit of Saul when he became disturbed internally and mentally over the prophecy of his loss of the kingdom. In due time, David had his contest with Goliath, the champion of the Philistines, and defeated him, thus gaining the attention of all Israel and having songs sung of him which praised him more than Saul. Immediately, David won the friendship of Jonathan, the son of Saul, and made with him a life covenant. He also won the love of Saul's daughter Michal and in due season became her husband. All these things raised the jealousy of Saul and stirred his antagonism. Because of his mental derangement, Saul attempted to kill David out of jealousy and David had to flee for his life. Though no evil could be found in him, he became an outlaw.

David's experiences as an outlaw reveal many trials to his faith. He was always but a step from death. Saul's men were pursuing him wherever he went and often the local people betrayed his whereabouts when he was hiding from Saul's army. Once in unbelief he departed from Israel and lived with the Philistines only to be compelled to lie in order to protect his own life and the lives of those who followed him. In all this, David's attitude toward God was revealed in the fact that he refused to kill Saul when Saul fell into his grasp on two occasions and he referred his cause unto the Lord as the God of vengeance and as the disposer of all events.

The Conditions Calling for Prudence

In the midst of David's wanderings, as he kept himself hidden from Saul and Saul's army, he and his 600 men abode in the wilderness of Paran. This was located in the rugged and forbidding mountains near unto Sinai in the southern peninsula east of the Sea of Akaba. To find David here would be like hunting for a partridge in the mountains. All Israel, including Abigail and Nabal, a wealthy sheep owner, knew of the situation between Saul and David. They also knew that David was not an outlaw in the common meaning of that term — namely, a violator of a nation's laws and a predator upon the property and possessions of peaceful citizens; rather, he was a protector of the poor and the exploited and the tyrannized. In fact, whenever an individual suffered injustice in the nation, as was common under the kingship of Saul, he fled and joined up with the band of men around David. David had to move his father and mother to Mizpah of Moab and committed them to the keeping of the king of Moab until he should see how conditions went with him (I Sam. 22:3, 4). Then, with his band of men, he dwelt in the wilderness of Engedi for a season, in the wilderness of Paran for a season, with the Philistines for a season, but always he attempted to protect and to defend the people of Israel and especially the poor. There is a very real parallel here between the actions of David during his years as an outlaw and the legendary actions of Robin Hood in Sherwood Forest of England. During the absence of Richard, king of England, the rulership of the realm was turned over to Prince John who attempted to establish himself as the permanent king of England and to exterminate the friends and supporters of his brother Richard. According to the legend, Robin Hood was one of these lords who was faithful to Richard but took to the forest where there gathered to him the exploited, the tyrannized and the victims of injustice of Prince John. He, too, protected the poor and attempted to rally sentiment for the true king of the land. By interpreting the acts of David during this season in the light of the legend of Robin Hood, we might understand it better.

In this background we are to recognize that the man Nabal, who had three thousand sheep and a thousand goats that grazed in this southern section of the Negeb near unto the wilderness of Paran, was in constant peril of loss of his possessions. He was in no peril from David and his men, but he was from beasts of the wilderness and also from robbers. His own servants testified of David and his men, saying, "The men were very good unto us, and we were not hurt, neither missed we any thing, as long as we were conversant with them, when we were in the fields: they were a wall unto us both by night and day, all the while we were with them keeping the sheep" (I Sam. 25:15, 16). David himself testified in sending greetings to Nabal, "Now thy shepherds which were with us, we hurt them not, neither was there ought missing unto them, all the while they were in Carmel. Ask thy young men, and they will shew thee." Here was a dual testimony to the beneficent actions of David and his men in reference to any Israelite who had possessions in the area in which he took refuge from the armies of Saul.

It was necessary, however, for David and his men to live and the time came when Nabal was to shear his three thousand sheep and his thousand goats, which was the source of his income and which had made him wealthy. At this time, Nabal had held a feast for his friends and his servants which was like the feast of a king (I Sam. 25:36). Quite properly, David, for the service which he had performed, sent an embassage of ten young men to Nabal to request whatever good thing Nabal should desire to give unto him and to his men for their sustenance. The principle involved here was that stated by Paul in I Corinthians and quoted from the Old Testament when he said, "Thou shalt not muzzle the mouth of the ox that treadeth out the corn" (I Cor. 9:9). The meaning is that if one serves, he should participate in the fruit of his service. If he labors, he should participate in the fruit of his labors. It was quite a legitimate thing for David to expect a gift from Nabal in recognition of his services and also of his need. The contrast here between asking and taking, or thieving, is definite. David had attempted to serve and now expected his reward.

Our text tells us that Nabal was churlish and evil in his doings. This is a rather strange comment because he was of the "house of Caleb" and the house of Caleb was noted for its perfect obedience of the Lord, for its leadership of the tribes of Israel during the period of the judges, and for its righteousness. But here, of the tribe of Caleb, was a man who was a fool. He was churlish in his spirit and he gave an insulting reply unto David. He answered David's men by saying, "Who is David? and who is the son of Jesse? there be many servants now a days that break away every man from his master. Shall I then take my bread, and my water, and my flesh that I have killed for my shearers, and give it unto men; whom I know not whence they be?" (I Sam. 25:10, 11). With this answer

David's ten young men went their way and carried their message to David.

What a case of folly this was! As Nabal's name, so his action. Nabal means folly and he was foolish in what he did. What man who is exposed to the depredations of a band of 600 hard-pressed and hungry outlaws would reject a moderate request for food in the light of service which had been performed for the man? David was in a position to do harm to Nabal at that time just as he could have done harm unto his flocks and herds all the time that he watched over them in the wilderness. Any man of normal judgment and sense of values would recognize that the prudent thing would have been to have made a gift unto David and his men and thanked them for their services. When the report of the embassage came to David, his indignation was stirred and he was full of wrath. He gave the command, "Gird ye on every man his sword," and, at the head of a band of 400, leaving 200 to abide by the stuff, David started to take vengeance upon Nabal and his household. His intention was stated unto Abigail when she met him. He said, "Surely in vain have I kept all that this fellow hath in the wilderness, so that nothing was missed of all that pertained unto him: and he hath requited me evil for good. So and more also do God unto the enemies of David, if I leave of all that pertain to him by the morning light."

There are certain ethical questions that arise in the Old Testament which do not seem to be reconcilable with the New Testament way of life for a believer. We find occasions when individuals like David, who for the sake of preserving their own lives, lie. Such were David's words unto Ahimelech, the priest, when he fled from Saul (I Sam. 21:2). Another illustration is that of making a foray against one's enemies and killing them and taking their stuff as a spoil. Such was David's activity when he raided the Geshurites and then lied about it to Achish, the king of Gath (I Sam. 27:8-12). Another illustration is that of the violation of the creation ordinance of monogamy. Men of the Old Testament often had more than one wife.

The best we can do in explaining these Old Testament

ethical problems is to evaluate and judge them in the light of the times in which they occurred and of the practices of those times. The Old Testament saints who transgressed the permanent and ultimate standard of morality of the Bible did so because of the limitation of revelation and because of the age in which they lived.

THE CHARACTERISTICS OF PRUDENCE

Prudence is a gift of understanding a situation and acting in accordance with it. Abigail, the wife of Nabal, was informed of Nabal's action to the embassage of David by one of the young shepherds who worked for Nabal. When he concluded his report he said, "For [Nabal] is such a son of Belial, that a man cannot speak to him." He warned Abigail that harm was impending to not only Nabal but his whole household from David because of Nabal's action. In a moment Abigail grasped the situation. She evaluated it correctly and determined to act to avert disaster to her household. With haste, she prepared a magnificent offering to David and to his men of bread, of wine, of sheep, of corn, of clusters of raisins, of cakes of figs, so that David and his men could also have a bounty fit for a king. With this laded upon donkeys, she made her way speedily toward the direction from which David and his men should come and she told not her husband. Abigail's understanding of the obligation of Nabal, of the peril in which the household lay, and of the way in which this peril could be averted, was most commendatory.

Prudence is conciliatory action. Abigail not only took her offering to demonstrate the attitude of her mind toward David, but she also went herself and determined she would conciliate David by an apology for Nabal, by a correct assessment of Nabal's character, and by a plea unto him to commit his way unto the Lord and not take it into his own hands. Had Abigail not taken action and had waited for David and his men to come unto Nabal's household, it would have been too late.

Prudence is also a humility of attitude. When Abigail saw David, she got down from the donkey, fell on the ground on her face before David, did obeisance to him, and then made her plea. There was no claiming of position, there was no castigation of David as an outlaw, there was no folly on her part. She recognized that she was a suppliant, that her life and the existence of her household depended upon the mercy which David would display. But she did say that she knew nothing of the coming of the messengers nor of their departure without goods and she offered the offering which she had brought as a magnificent evidence of her good will toward David.

Prudence is also wisdom of counsel. In Abigail's plea she pointed out unto David that God had restrained him from avenging himself and shedding blood, thus from corrupting his record in Israel. He was known as the great protector of the poor and had he exterminated Nabal's household, he would have lost this position among the people. She also reminded him that the believer should commit his way unto God, that God is the great avenger. "Vengeance is mine; I will repay, saith the Lord." Therefore, she told David that he should praise the Lord that He had kept him from avenging himself with his own hands and she pointed out that the Lord will certainly care for him because his life was as a bundle of life bound up with the life of God and that God would take care of his enemies. Abigail actually expressed David's own convictions and described the way David had lived up until that point and her counsel was recognized by David as coming from the Lord.

In this we may get a glimpse of what a woman may do for a man in being a wise counselor or being a prudent wife. Many a man has found that a woman has expressed his own convictions, restrained him from violating them and confirmed them in his determination to do the will of God.

The Consequence of Prudence

David accepted the counsel of Abigail. He said, "Blessed be the Lord God of Israel, which sent thee this day to meet me: and blessed be thy advice, and blessed be thou, which hast

kept me this day from coming to shed blood, and from avenging myself with mine own hand." David recognized the wisdom, the understanding and the righteousness of Abigail's counsel. Here was a woman who spoke as a prophetess of the Lord.

Abigail's person was also admired. Incidentally, as David
recognized what Abigail had done and the wisdom which had
motivated her action, his eyes were not closed to her beauty
and the comeliness of her person. This was evidenced from
the fact that as soon as Nabal had been smitten by the Lord
with a disease which took his life and the word came to David,
he remembered Abigail and sent to take her as his wife. The
fact that at the meeting David received of her hand that which
she brought him and sent her away in peace and said, "I . . .
have accepted thy person" was an assurance unto Abigail.

Abigail's life then was identified with the life of David.
When he sent to take her as his wife, he was still an outlaw.
They which sought his life would seek her life. Her situation
would depend entirely upon the situation of David, thus she
was in safeguard with him. As a result, she and the other
members of David's party of 600 who were not armed men
were captured at Ziklag and taken into captivity only to be
rescued by David and his four hundred. Later, when David
was accepted as the king of Judah at Hebron, Abigail became
the queen and later yet she became the mother of Chileab, his
second born son. Her life was the fruit of truth.

10

Bathsheba

The Woman Who Was Betrayed

> *And David sent and inquired after this woman and one*
> *said, 'Is not this Bath-sheba, the daughter of Eliam, the*
> *wife of Uriah the Hittite?* (II Sam. 11:3).

The meaning of "betrayal" is customarily associated with
the betrayal of a woman by a man through falseness, but this
is not the only means of betrayal. One, however, would naturally associate such with the title of this chapter. Evidently
there was much of this falseness of man to woman in the law-
less times represented by certain sections of the Bible. As the
human race degenerated, more and more women were treated
lightly and as a plaything of man, to be violated when he
pleased. These heathen practices sometimes affected Israel
and seeped into the national life of the people of God. Under
the advice of Balaam in the matter of Beth Peor, the Israelites
were led into great sin through this practice (Num. 25; 31:16),
but the Hebrew laws expressly forbade it, and they correctly
divided responsibility between the man and the woman so that
through the respective punishments this practice should be
utterly wiped out from the commonwealth of the people of
God. Such sin was called "folly in Israel."

There were, however, numerous examples of this folly.
Once Dinah, the daughter of Jacob, went to visit the daughters
of the land in Shechem, where the Israelites were sojourning
in their wanderings. There she was found by a prince of the
land, the son of Hamor, and was betrayed by him. The wrong

111

was so keenly felt by the sons of Jacob that they, in turn, through trickery, were enabled to avenge themselves upon the whole of the city and, unreasonably, they slew all the males in the city, an act strongly condemned by Jacob himself (Gen. 34). Another incident is that of Amnon and Tamar (II Sam. 13). Tamar was the beautiful sister of Absalom, the favorite son of David. Her half-brother, Amnon, loved her and, through the advice of a child of Belial, was able to betray her. Again it was called "folly in Israel," and this time it was punished with death. Absalom invited his brother Amnon and the other brothers of the kingly family to a feast and during the feast Amnon was slain; everyone knew that it was because he had wronged Absalom's sister. Yet as we read the history of the people of Israel over a period of sixteen hundred years, we are amazed that there are so remarkably few incidents of this in the narrative. Wherever they appear, it is with strong condemnation from the Hebrew law.

The last great case was that of David and Bath-sheba. It becomes the outstanding example in the Bible, one filled with many lessons for those who will study it. God certainly did not put this in the Bible in order that it might be suppressed in our thinking and teaching. However, had it not appeared in the Bible, no minister would ever presume to select it out of any other type of literature in order to make it a topic of a sermon, for it contains dreadful sins. Alexander Whyte says that it is in the Bible in order that we might realize that even the heroes of the faith are men of like passions as we are, to show us that the saints were not so far above us but we, in turn, can rise to their level.

> *Not in their brightness, but their earthly stains,*
> *Are the true scenes vouchsafed to earthly eyes,*
> *And saints are lowered that the world may rise.*

Under the word "betrayal" there is also the thought that immediately comes to one of the betrayal of one's country or of one's friends. Especially is this so at the Passion season of Christ, when we are thinking of the great drama centered around His person and the betrayal that concerned Him. Cer-

tainly the act of Judas of selling his Lord and Master to the
Jews in order that they might accuse Him and turn Him over
to the Romans to be put to death is the acme of faithlessness
we consider under the word "betrayal." Truly Jesus "was
wounded in the house of His friends." He even called Judas
"friend" in the Garden when he kissed Him in order to designate Him as the One whom the soldiers were to apprehend
(Matt. 26:49, 50). Many men through history have taken
their places with Judas in our estimation. There is, for one,
Benedict Arnold, who for a miserable sum and a promise of
station in British life, sold the secrets of his country to an
enemy. Though the early exploits of Arnold were of great
heroism and patriotism, nevertheless this stain upon his character forever brands him as an outcast in the thinking of true
Americans. Following him, there was Aaron Burr, who was
accused of conceiving a means of treason by which a large
section of the United States would fall to a foreign country
over which he, in turn, ultimately might preside. These were
acts of betrayal large enough to be noted by all men; but there
are many acts of betrayal that are accomplished daily and of
denials both to Christ and to our friends that should brand
many men as traitors and as faithless. These do not become
generally known.

One of the commonest acts of betrayal in life is that of a
woman by a woman. Well did Paul say that the younger
women should marry and bear children and guide the house
and give none occasion to the adversary to speak reproach-
fully (I Tim. 5:14), for he said he had learned that some of
them wandered about from house to house and were not only
idle but tattlers also, and busybodies, speaking things which
they ought not. He went even farther and said that no man
should ever be elected a deacon whose wife was given to
slander. Some of the most terrible wounds that are ever given
to men and women are given in the house of their friends
through the use of the tongue. Why women in particular are
subject to petty ambitions, jealousies, and envies of life is hard
to know, but experience has certainly vindicated the truth of

the teaching of the apostle Paul. Sometimes even professing Christians will allow these petty things to assume mountainous size and, though they act as friends to the faces of their women acquaintances, they do the most dastardly lying through innuendo, gossip, and slander behind their backs. This seems to be one of the devil's favorite pastimes, but all women who are tempted to engage in such sin or who have already engaged in it should be warned that justice will avenge them as surely as it avenged the action of Judas or of Benedict Arnold or of David or of anyone else guilty of betrayal. The reaping begins immediately with the act in lowering the character of the gossiper or the slanderer. The law, "whatsoever you sow you will also reap" (Gal. 6:7), immediately comes into operation.

I. The Woman Who Was Betrayed

It has been the habit when thinking of Bath-sheba to think of the sinfulness of David in betraying her, and no one would ever excuse David for his actions in this case. His soul must have been as dark as night and his action as culpable as anything that Satan ever did, but in spite of it, David was not the only one who sinned. It is this fact that has often been overlooked. We learn sufficient about Bath-sheba from the story to justify us in passing a judgment upon her conduct, for certainly she was an accomplice of David in this sin.

Bath-sheba's responsibility lay in three things. First, she was immodest, or David would never have been led to the sin. Second, she submitted to David's desire without any protest. Third, she concealed the event from her own husband, Uriah. Whenever a woman is deliberately immodest, she brings upon herself the judgment of salacious recklessness. In order to understand this in the case of Bath-sheba, one must know a bit about the construction of houses in Jerusalem in that ancient day. There the roofs were all flat and were commonly used as a place of refreshment in the cool evening air for the inhabitants of the city. Since the houses were closely joined one to another, any commanding eminence could overlook the roofs of other houses. Evidently David's palace was near by the home of Uriah and overlooked its roof. Certainly all this was known to Bath-sheba, and yet she mounted to the roof of her house at eventide and, with a possibility that she would be seen by someone from the roof of an adjoining house, she publicly exposed herself. Granting that this was mere immodesty and not a deliberate act upon her part, we still hold that Bath-sheba was responsible for a definite part in the sin of David, for it was at that moment that David was walking upon the roof of the palace and he beheld her and had awakened in him the temptation to which he succumbed.

Next we read that when David sent messengers to bring Bath-sheba to the palace, she came. Moreover, we have recorded no conversation, no remonstrance, merely a rapid passing over of the events that became the cause of his later crime. Yet when we turn to a heathen queen such as Vashti, in the time of Ahasuerus, we are told that when she was commanded to be immodest and to present herself before the banquet of the king, she refused, even at the cost of her throne (Esther 1:10-12). Ahasuerus was of a greater power as an Oriental monarch than even David, for David was compelled to act according to law. Having heard no outcry, having no record of any resistance or any remonstrance on the part of Bath-sheba, we may assume that she submitted voluntarily to the act and thus she could not be without guilt.

Third, when Bath-sheba's husband, Uriah, was called home from the battle front by David and slept by the door of David's house, Bath-sheba sent him no word nor did she even communicate with him personally to tell him what had happened, to denounce the king, and to confess with tearful eyes and with a grieved soul of the shame that had been wrought upon her. It seems that she even condescended to the plan of David of disposing of her husband in order that she might be added to the harem of the king. A careful reading of this narrative, which in part lays the great blame upon David, and rightly so, will leave one with the impression that Bath-sheba certainly was not without her sin as an accomplice in this act.

For this reason, Bath-sheba was not without her suffering.

After Uriah was dead and she had been married to the king and the child who had been conceived in sin was born, God struck the child and it was very sick. David was so moved by the suffering of Bath-sheba and by his own love for the child that he fasted and wept and prayed and lay upon the earth seven days without eating or drinking in order to gain the mercy of God for the child (II Sam. 12:15-17). If this is a description of what David did, what must have been happening in the case of Bath-sheba? Undoubtedly in this experience she recognized the hand of God chastening her for her part in the sin. We may well imagine the grief of her soul, the tears that flowed, the prayers she uttered, the contrition she manifested, and then the sorrow in the death of the child. The Lord was to punish David still farther, but the primary punishment of the beautiful woman, Bath-sheba, came to her in connection with the loss of this little one, who had already entwined his fingers around her heart.

Many years later an event occurred in the life of David — just before his death — that tells us David made compensation and restitution to Bath-sheba for the wrong he had done. He may have done it in the days of her suffering because of the loss of the child. David was now an old man and Adonijah, his son, had declared that he was king. Then Nathan sent Bath-sheba to converse with the king about Solomon, her son, and she said, "My lord, thou swearest by the Lord thy God unto thine handmaid, saying, assuredly Solomon thy son shall reign after me, and he shall sit upon my throne" (I Kings 1:17). Then the king answered Bath-sheba with an oath, saying, "As the Lord liveth, that hath redeemed my soul out of all distress, even as I sware unto thee by the Lord God of Israel, saying, assuredly Solomon thy son shall reign after me, and he shall sit upon my throne in my stead; even so will I certainly do this day." Sometime in this early relationship, when under contrition, sorrow, remorse, and even repentance this couple suffered, David with an oath swore unto God that he would make this compensation to Bath-sheba. It had been so long past that he had almost forgotten it, but undoubtedly it was done in order to lessen her suffering. However we look upon Bath-sheba, whether as one who was innocent or guilty, she suffered severely from this wrong.

II. The Man Who Betrayed Her

The Bible is exceedingly candid in revealing the sins of the heroes of the faith. In any other book but the Bible, where the biography of this man was being presented, this would have been suppressed, but the Bible tells this incident in its greatest detail. Here was a man, called a man after God's own heart, yet one who fell terribly and sinned grievously in the sight of God. Surely this, instead of being an evidence against the Bible as the Word of God, is an example of its inspiration, for by means of this event the divine mercy and judgment were revealed and demonstrated in behalf of man. The fact that God knows everything and suppresses nothing and has said that everything will be made known, even that which is hidden here on earth, ought to bring stark fear to the hearts of some people for taking comfort in covering the sins in which they have indulged. There is only one way to be safe after you have sinned, and this is to confess that sin and openly acknowledge it in the sight of God and of those whom you have wronged in order that it may forever be put away from you.

There were definite steps in David's fall which may be of value to us in warning and teaching. His temptation came to him at a time when kings went forth to battle. The Bible implies that David should have been at the head of his armies in the siege of Rabbah instead of languishing at ease in his palace in Jerusalem. A long process of inner corruption must have already taken place in David to weaken him and make him ready for such a fall, and that process is shown by the fact that he was taking his ease when Israel dwelt in tents. Uriah emphasized this when David urged him to go to his home and sent a mess of meat after him that he might enjoy himself. Said he, "The ark, and Israel, and Judah, abide in tents; and my lord Joab, and the servants of my lord, are encamped in the open fields; shall I then go into mine house, to eat and to drink . . . as thy soul liveth, I will not do this thing" (II Sam. 11:11). Uriah had the attitude David should have had. Next, when David saw the object of temptation, instead of immediately putting it from his mind, he toyed with it as a thought until he was consumed with desire and driven to action. However, he then excused himself; he had a right as an absolute monarch to do this thing; since he had lived so close to God during his whole life he could now afford one indulgence. He, nevertheless, knew that it was contrary to the will of God who had established him upon his throne, and he deliberately sinned. Just one such sin is able to spoil the entire life of a saint of God and bring him low. In one instant, one can undo the work of a lifetime. By one fall, the influence we exercised over many may be completely ruined.

The resulting sin was of so shocking a character that we cannot dwell upon it. It is horrible and repulsive and it ought not even to be associated with the name of a man after God's own heart. It was an act of ignominious adultery of the plainest kind. Secondly, it included the act of intoxicating his friend in an effort to conceal his own guilt (II Sam. 11:13). Third, when this artifice failed, it included the deliberate murder of an innocent and faithful officer of his army. It was the concealing of his sin even more than the sin itself which, according to the Scripture, displeased the Lord.

During the period that followed, David's condition was anything but pleasant. It lasted approximately twelve months — from the time of his sin until the time of the revelation of that sin. This has been called by Bishop Butler a time of self-deceit in the life of David. It cannot be overlooked that it was after a year of deceit, internal hypocrisy, and self-forgiving silence on David's part that Nathan was sent to David with the message of divine indignation. "How a man like David could have lived all that time soaked to the eyes in adultery and murder and not go mad is simply inconceivable." Bishop Butler goes on to show how that this self-deception is the heart of the sin of each of us. We condone ourselves when we judge others.

This may be the reason that David was so intensely and unusually cruel in his treatment of the people of Rabbah when they were conquered by the armies of Israel. However we interpret the verse that describes this, it still is a cruel treatment (II Sam. 12:31). While we condone our own sins, we are often severe judges of others. Moreover, when Nathan came to David with his parable of an unjust, wealthy man who stole the lamb from the poor man, David's wrath flashed in righteous indignation. He was hypocritically showing himself to be a righteous judge of others while completely excusing himself.

The Scripture says that this sin of David gave occasion for the enemies of the Lord to blaspheme (II Sam. 12:14). There are many things in the narrative concerning Joab that would lead us to believe that he was a true believer. On the other hand, there are many things that lead us to believe that he was not. David commanded his son Solomon that after his death Joab should be judged for his sins he had done of murder of innocent men, and Joab was put to death (I Kings 2:5, 6). I suppose that when Joab learned of this particular sin of David, he then was able the more readily to excuse himself for the wrongs that he had done. Then there was Shimei, who cursed David and who was wicked in heart (II Sam. 16:5-14). There was Ziba, the servant of Mephibosheth, who had done wrong (II Sam. 16:1-4; 19:25-30), and I suppose the kingdom was full of evil-doers who now took comfort for the things that they had done that were wrong because the king had set them the standard and had excused himself for at least a year. This is something of an example of what sins of believers do in the church and to the world. Whenever someone who professes to be a leader in the church is guilty of a wicked violation of God's law and covers it up, though the world knows about it, he sets the example for others and helps them along the road to hell. Better is it by far that we should judge ourselves and cleanse ourselves from all iniquity than to set a stumbling-block in the way of someone else.

III. The Betrayer in the Hands of God

After it was evident that David was to excuse, to forgive, and to condone himself for the things that he had done by one argument or another, and that he would not be led to confession and repentance through his own self-judgment, God sent a messenger to him, the prophet Nathan. To be pointed at and to be told to his face that he was unclean and cruel and cowardly and guilty of blood was David's salvation. "To have someone injured enough and angry enough, or friendly and honest enough and kind enough to call you to your face false, or cruel, or envious, or malicious, or hard-hearted, or ignorant and narrow-minded and full of prejudice and party spirit, or meek to the great and harsh to the poor, or all that together, might be the beginning of your salvation." Such a person, instead of being your enemy, would be your greatest friend. The Scripture says, "Let the righteous smite me; it shall be a kindness: and let him reprove me; it shall be an excellent oil, which shall not break my head" (Ps. 141:5). Thus it was that Nathan came with his story saying, "There were two men in one city; the one rich, and the other poor. The rich man had exceeding many flocks and herds: but the poor man had nothing, save one little ewe lamb, which he had bought and nourished up: and it grew up together with him, and with his children; it did eat of his own meat, and drank of his own cup, and lay in his bosom, and was unto him as a daughter. And there came a traveler unto the rich man, and he spared to take of his own flock and of his own herd, to dress for the wayfaring man that was come unto him; but he took the poor man's lamb, and dressed it for the man that was come to him" (II Sam. 12:1-4). To this picture of domestic happiness and beauty there came tragedy—stark, cruel, awful tragedy—and it struck David's sense of pity and of justice. In wrath David cried, "As the Lord liveth, the man that hath done this thing shall surely die: and he shall restore the lamb fourfold, because he did this thing, and because he had no pity." Little did David know that the sword of God's justice and judgment was hanging within but a hairbreadth of his own head. But now it began to cut his conscience. Said Nathan, "Thou art the man. You were the king of Israel and possessed riches and comforts, palaces, servants, wives, slaves and concubines, and if that had been too little, I would have given thee such and such things. Wherefore, then, hast thou despised the commandment of the Lord to do evil in His sight? Thou hast killed Uriah the Hittite with the sword and taken his wife to be thy wife, and thou hast slain him with the sword of the children of Ammon." How much better it would have been for David had he allowed his own conscience to smite him first, to play the part of God and the part of Nathan the prophet! How much better for him had he confessed these things privately, before they were revealed publicly and he was made an object lesson for the Lord! Even so, it is better for us today to take our sins out and confess them openly and make restitution before that which is hidden is revealed in the justice of an infinite God. The wisdom and delicacy of Nathan in preaching this sermon to David is very beautiful. Often we thunder and we blunder and we fail to lead men to repentance, but before David even knew it, the sword of the Word of God lodged itself in his heart and rather than turn against his friend Nathan for preaching against him, he turned against himself and condemned himself in the eyes of God. Surely when Nathan made that speech to David, he was but a step from death, for an Oriental monarch could have confined him easily to the dungeon or commanded his death, but instead, David said, "I have sinned against the Lord" (II Sam. 12:13).

David's repentance was immediate. As soon as he saw himself as God saw him, as a pitiless, selfish, and heartless monarch, as one who had everything and yet spared not another man's little, he cried out in self-loathing, aversion, and confession of his sin. This whole story is unlike the noble, blessed David of the Old Testament whom we know and love. Deep in his heart he was not this way, and as soon as he saw himself as God now saw him, he was smitten in heart and repented. There were no excuses given by David now. There was no false repentance. There was no condoning of self.

There was only a sense of transgression. Just as quickly as David repented, God forgave him, for Nathan said, "The Lord also hath put away thy sin; thou shalt not die. Howbeit . . ." Then he went on to tell of the punishment that would come upon David.

Because David had given the enemies of the Lord occasion to blaspheme by his act, therefore, the enemies of the Lord must see that David should suffer at the hands of a righteous God for the things that he had done. The first punishment that should come upon him was that the sword would never depart from his house. What an awful prediction this was for a man whose throne God had promised to establish forever and ever! First, we see the sword as it flashes in the hands of Absalom, killing his brother Amnon for what he did to Tamar (II Sam. 13). Next we see the sword flashing in the hands of Joab as it pierced the heart of Absalom while he hung in the tree (II Sam. 18:14). Again we see the sword flashing as thousands rose in revolt against the old King David. Suffering, death, and destruction came into his family as a punishment of God. Second, the Lord said, "I will raise up evil against thee out of thine own house." Never from this day until his death did David have a peaceful moment, without evil coming from one hand or another. While he was driven from the city of Jerusalem to take refuge in the wilderness from the revolt of his own son Absalom, he was cursed by Shimei, who went along throwing dust in the air and calling him a bloody man. When some of the host wanted to go up and slay Shimei, David said, "Let him alone. The Lord hath told him to curse me. Maybe the Lord will have mercy upon me." David knew that the evil had come to him by way of retribution. Third, God said, "I will take thy wives before thine eyes and give them unto thy neighbor, and it shall be done in the sight of this sun, for thou didst it secretly, but I will do this thing before Israel." David had taken another man's wife and secretly violated her, and now the wives of his own household were violated in the eyes of the public by Absalom, his own son (II Sam. 16:22). The law of sowing and reaping was completely fulfilled in these characters, David and Bath-sheba. Thus anyone who sins against the Lord by the betrayal of the Lord or the betrayal of a friend or the betrayal of his ideals should tremble with the thought of what God will do to him. Punishment will inevitably come to him in the end. As truly as there is justice and goodness at the heart of the universe, all that is contrary to justice and goodness must either be forgiven through the cross or be punished by suffering.

In a magnificent sermon upon this subject, Dr. C. E. Macartney describes how the heavenly host were filled with sorrow at the fall of David. The angels refused even the music of their harps during the time between David's fall and David's repentance. One angel said to the other, "Take thine harp and give me melody this day," but the angel answered, "I cannot sing, for David, the man after God's own heart, the man who stole the music of heaven and set it to vibrating among the sons of men, is fallen." But when the tidings came that David had repented and that he had said, "Against Thee, Thee only, have I sinned, and done this evil in Thy sight. Cast me not away from Thy presence; and take not Thy Holy Spirit from me" (Ps. 51:4, 11), then there was joy in heaven again. Every harp was lifted and every tongue was loosed in praise of Him who turns the hearts of kings as waters of rivers are turned. There is joy in heaven over one sinner who repenteth. What joy there must have been over the repentance of David.

You who are women, ask yourself right now whether you have been guilty of sins that will affect others and lead them into temptation and evil. If you are a man, have you ever betrayed another man, or have you betrayed your Lord or the principles of your Lord? If any one of us has sinned in one way or another, have we waited until God should send us another to convict us of our sin? Why not take the Word as it is given to us tonight and apply it to our hearts, bow in His presence, confessing the evil we have done, and then make restitution thereof before the time of judgment comes? Forgiveness is with Him.

11

The Shunammite

The Woman Whose Hospitality Was Rewarded

And he said, About this season, according to the time of life, thou shalt embrace a son (II Kings 4:16).

This story of the hospitable Shunammite is a parable upon all those who are in desperation concerning their children. The Shunammite needed help from the prophet because the child whom God had given to her had an accident and died. Most people stand in need of help for their children, not because of accident, illness or death, but because of moral problems such as violence, crime and sex.

Parents are perplexed, distressed and helpless in the face of the revolt, transgression and intemperance of youth. These young people have rejected all authority, restraint and control by their parents. It is now a common thing for graduates from high school to stay up all night either on the night of their graduation or the night of their senior prom. Even otherwise very well trained and integrated young people seem to be impelled by the mass spirit to live dangerously and to do things which they otherwise would not do. The repudiation of chaperonage, the demand for freedom and action, and the resort to antisocial actions are becoming far more prevalent than we like to admit. Insurance companies and newspapers report the rising accident rate in the use of automobiles by those under twenty-one.

In addition, social agencies report the increase of immorality and illegitimacy in the high-school age. The secretary of the Child Welfare Agency of the N. A. E. declared that the age of unmarried mothers was becoming lower and lower until even 12-year-olds were involved. The juvenile delinquency resulting in crime and violence is now deplored over the whole nation. It seems impossible to pick up the morning paper without reading about a murder perpetrated by some boy or girl on a companion, a parent or stranger. One principal of a high school was driven to suicide by the pressure of these juvenile delinquents in his own school. The looseness of morals in many college communities has reached a new high.

All of this reflects a failure on the part of an older generation but presents a problem with which we have to deal. The juvenile problem has arisen from too many working women, too many broken homes, too many orphan families, too much drinking, too much loose living, and too much pleasure seeking. Self-discipline and discipline of families have gone from American life. Our parents stand in great need of help with their children.

One source of help that can be given is a change in the laws of our nation which deal with the education and working habits of youth. There was a time when child labor laws were necessary to prevent the exploitation of youth by unprincipled employers. These laws have now made it necessary to keep young people in school until they are 16 or 18 when they would be far better off working in some creative activity or some responsible duty. When a child has no aptitude or desire for education beyond a certain stage, say junior high school, he ought not to be compelled by law to remain in school but should be permitted to go to work. It is a tragedy for any nation when its children become evil doers. Compare Isaiah 1:4, 5.

But a far greater source of help to parents in dealing with the needs of their children today rests in knowing where to turn for such help and in finding it in God's truth, in Jesus Christ and in Christian fellowship. With this in mind, let us look at the story of the hospitable Shunammite woman for instruction.

with them or in preparing for them a prophet's chamber, or in meeting their other needs!

This was "a little chamber" but it was apart from the world. It reminds us of the invitation the Lord gave, "Come, my people, enter thou into thy chambers, and shut thy doors about thee: hide thyself as it were for a little moment" (Isa. 26:20). This little chamber was to have in it "a bed" for the rest of God's servant. It was the divine intention that His disciples should come apart and rest awhile. When the Lord Jesus invites us to come to Him, it is to find rest, not to be overburdened or overtired. The little chamber had in it "a table" which is a place of fellowship and of communion (I Cor. 1:9). It had in it "a stool" which is a place of humility, study and learning (Luke 10:38-42). The little chamber had in it "a candlestick" which symbolizes a testimony (Matt. 5:14-16). The little chamber was "on the wall" where the watchman was normally lodged, suggesting that the prophet is a watchman unto Israel (Ezek. 33:1-11). In all this, Elisha did not have much from the viewpoint of the world for he had exchanged wealth for it. When he plowed, it had been in the last of a series of 12 yoke of oxen on his father's farm, which reveals that his father was a man of wealth (I Kings 19:19). Many are the servants of the Lord who have given up much to sacrifice and work in God's vineyard.

The contributions which the Shunammite made was for God's sake. She said to her husband, "I perceive that this is an holy man of God." Her love and her loyalty were to Jehovah and only incidentally expressed unto Elisha as gratitude to Jehovah. Even the Lord Jesus commanded His disciples in their evangelistic travels to stay in the houses of those who were worthy and there abide until they departed from the city. This advice from Jesus was misused and in the Didache, or the teaching of the twelve, a warning was raised against anyone who tarried in someone's house too long. The action of the Shunammite was for "God's sake." Thus, the hospitality, generosity and service which we do should be for Christ's sake.

A good illustration of this in the Old Testament is found

in David's treatment of Mephibosheth, the son of Jonathan. After David was established king, he asked, "Is there not yet any of the house of Saul, that I may shew the kindness of God unto him?" (II Sam. 9). Upon investigation, Mephibosheth was found who was lame in both his feet, but David elevated him to sit at the king's table for the rest of his life because he was the son of Jonathan. This Shunammite's ministry and interest in Elisha were without any ulterior motive. She did not desire anything from him when she expressed her hospitality. This is reminiscent of the service and worship of Job who loved and served God for God's sake and not for what God did for him. Yet when Satan would accuse Job, he said, "Doth Job fear God for nought?" Yet Job's subsequent trial proved that he had no ulterior motive in his worship.

THE WOMAN'S HEART'S DESIRE

On one occasion when Elisha was using the room on the wall as his place of rest and study, he was so appreciative of it that he decided that she should do something for the Shunammite woman. Hence, he commanded Gehazi to call her unto him. As the woman stood before him he asked. "What is to be done for thee? wouldest thou be spoken for to the King, or to the captain of the host?" Elisha's heart was so filled with gratitude that he thought that he must confer upon this woman some manifestation of his appreciation. With noble disdain, the woman responded, "I dwell among mine own people," meaning that she had no need, had no desire, had no ulterior motive. With this she made her exit from the chamber. Hers was truly a disinterested piety and service which was done for God's sake. Others might have taken advantage of the prophet's request and have asked for some favor with the king or with the captain of the host. After the woman had gone Elisha offhandedly said to Gehazi, "What then is to be done for her?" the servant revealed his intuition and perception by saying, "Verily she hath no child, and her husband is old." In this he put his finger upon the deep desire of this woman's heart for a child.

Immediately Elisha commanded Gehazi to summon her. We can picture her as she responded, came to the door of the ·little room, and stood there awaiting the prophet's word. Little did she know what a blessing her hospitality was to bring her. Elisha said, "About this season, according to the time of life, thou shalt embrace a son." Here was a woman who had waited through her married life for a child and received none. Now, like Sarah who reached an advanced age before Isaac was born, or like Hannah, who was barren until God undertook for her and gave her Samuel, or like Elizabeth who had no longer hopes for a child when she was advanced in age, God now met the desire of this woman in promising her a child. Her deep satisfaction in receiving the promise is revealed by her incredulity in which she said, "Nay, my lord, thou man of God, do not lie unto thine handmaid." Hers was a sincere questioning in the light of the conditions but she nevertheless believed.

The text moves on immediately to the fulfillment of the promise (vs. 17). The day came when the child was born into that Shunammite household. What a celebration took place in the estate! The little town of Shunem rang for joy as the neighbors and fellow townspeople joined in with the happy Shunammite father and mother in the gift which God had made to them. All of the Shunammite woman's desires had centered in this gift, and now she was completely content with her blessing. Life was full for a number of years, and how fast those years passed as she trained that little child, taught him what she knew, exercised her creative influence, molded his character and directed his thought until the time came, "when the child was grown." Little do people realize the joys that they have in the days when their children are young, for they soon come when they are no longer under their control and when the problems multiply.

The Woman's Help Received

When the child was grown, that is, when he reached an age that he could run about for himself, pass in and out of the walls of the town, accompany his father into the fields, and take part in either the planting or harvesting, a sad and tragic accident took place. Whether he suffered from sunstroke, or brain hemorrhage, or some other thing, we know not, but he cried out, "My head, my head." His father was busy, so he commanded a lad to carry him to his mother. When she received him, she gathered him into her arms and held him upon her knees until at noontime he died.

What tragedy can strike in a believing household! Recently I attended a funeral for the daughter of an intimate friend. This man is a manager of an estate worth upward of a hundred million dollars. His daughter was a beautiful girl, seventeen years of age, and about to graduate from high school. She took an active part in Youth for Christ, was a soul winner and daily had her devotions of Bible reading and prayer. However, the week before her graduation she was riding with her boy friend to a neighboring town. A car which had been following her testified that the boy was driving at 45 miles an hour and on the right side of the road. Suddenly, another car, driven by two drunken marines, careened around a curve at 85 miles an hour. It smashed into this car and instantly killed the daughter and her boy friend. It was found that on the day before she was killed she had turned in a theme in her high school in answer to an assignment on "My Philosophy of Life." At the services which were held for her and which were attended by upward of a thousand people, this testimony was read. It displayed her as a mature Christian and a soul winner. I give it for your inspiration. It symbolizes what tragedies can strike, even in a Christian home.

"My philosophy of life is based on the Holy Bible and the God that wrote it. I know that He has a plan for my life and through daily prayer and reading of His Word I will be able to see it. As far as my life work or life partner, I am leaving it in His hands and am willing to do anything He says.

"I feel that this philosophy is very practical and can be applied to everyday life. Every decision can be taken to the Lord in prayer and the peace that comes from knowing Jesus Christ as my personal Saviour is something many cannot un-

derstand. Many search for a purpose and reason for life. I
know that I am on this earth to have fellowship with God and
to win others to the saving knowledge of His Son, Jesus Christ.
I know that after death I will go to be with Him forever.

"Jesus Christ teaches love and respect for everyone
throughout the New Testament and we are not to judge anyone because He will on the judgment day. In God's sight no
one person is worth any more than another.

"Knowing and loving Jesus Christ personally makes me
want to please Him and accomplish things for His glory. Paul
says in the New Testament, 'Whatsoever ye do, do all to the
glory of God,' and 'For me to live is Christ, and to die is gain.'

"This philosophy contains all of the seven points given in
your lecture of April 20th. As I stated in the beginning, it is
very (1) practical to have someone to turn to for any decision
or problem, small or large. What could be more (2) optimistic
than knowing that God has a purpose and plan for one's life
and is willing to keep in constant fellowship with anyone who
will. To know I have accepted Jesus Christ's gift of salvation
and will have eternal life in heaven is a most wonderful thing
and brings peace to my heart. God has the best for us and if
we let Him He will improve our lives and solve our problems.
(3) God in His Holy Word teaches us to have love and a burden for every person as Jesus Christ Himself. (4) One of my
main purposes in life is to share this experience I have had
with Christ and to show them the peace and happiness that it
brings. (5) This is an important goal in itself, but more completely, my aim in life is to accomplish what the Lord has for
me to do; which is certainly the most worthwhile goal in life.
(6) The closer I grow to Him the more happiness I find and
the busier I am. He has things for me that the world could
never offer and I learn to appreciate more and more how for-
tunate I am. (7) God's standards are higher than anything
attainable and present a great challenge and make me realize
how futile it would be for me to do the best I could, because I,
being human, could never reach God's standards, and there-

fore never be worthy of entering heaven. God has given me contact with the best; in His world, in my born-again friends, and in my fellowship with Jesus Christ. It is well known that the highest beauty, truth, justice and goodness is found in God's Word.

"This is my philosophy, and yet it is not mine, but I am God's and whatever I have is His and I have faith that He is the only answer and I do love Him so."

But often things worse than death can come unto the children of believers. In the trial for rape in Tallahassee, Florida, the Christian mother of one of the defendants wept as she told of her attempting to train her boy, send him to Sunday school and to lead him in the right way. Yet, he was involved in this terrible crime which ordinarily would draw the death penalty in Florida. One thinks of the youthful slayings in different areas in this country and of the sorrows which are caused to the parents. Those who are faced with such tragedies can find comfort in one thing alone, that is, in knowing where to turn as did the Shunammite woman (vss. 21-25). She turned to Elisha and to Elisha's God, for she knew that He alone would be able to meet her need.

When the Shunammite came to Elisha, he perceived her sorrow and burden and said, "Let her alone; for her soul is vexed within her: and the Lord hath hid it from me." This picture of the vexed soul of this Shunammite woman is a picture of countless fathers and mothers who have been vexed over the tragedies which have befallen their children. Just recently a woman with three children wrote me about one of her boys who had been brought up by her to go to Sunday school, to do odd chores, to attend the regular school and to be faithful. Suddenly he repudiated the church, he took up with evil companions, he began staying out late, he drank liquor and finally was guilty of a crime. The distraught cry of that vexed mother was like unto the distraught soul of this Shunammite. All who have had their children struck down by illegitimacy, shame, prison sentence or crime share that sorrow.

Yet succor was given unto this woman by Elisha. Her

faith is displayed in her answer to Gehazi when he was instructed by Elisha to ask her, "Is it well with thee? is it well with thy husband? is it well with the child?" and she answered, "It is well." She believed that Elisha had the answer for her problem. Let there be faith on the part of parents that God does have the answer for their problem. I think of the transformation in a teen-age boy who, in his home in Arizona, belonged to a gang who fought with other gangs composed of Mexicans and half-breeds, using brass knuckles, billies and other instruments of violence. But his parents prayed for him, brought him into contact with other young people who knew Christ so that he heard the Gospel and was converted. He was taken out, put in a Christian school and then ultimately sent to Wheaton College where he became a leader in the college and student life. God had met the need of those parents.

When the Shunammite woman came to Elisha, she fell at his feet and clasped them in her arms in fervent petition that he would help her. Gehazi would have thrust her away but Elisha said, "Let her alone," for he realized that there was a deep and persistent need in her life. She would not be satisfied with the ministries of Gehazi or any lesser servant but only that of Elisha.

The response, therefore, came in Elisha's going to her home, praying for the child, resuscitating it so that the child could be presented to her alive. Only a spiritual resurrection or rebirth of those in moral and spiritual need is the answer to the problems faced by parents today. When such resuscitation comes, the need may easily be met.

The woman served the Lord with disinterested piety exemplified in hospitality to His servant. As a result, she received a reward in help for her own family and her own son.

12

The Queen of Sheba

THE WOMAN WHO MADE HISTORY

> And she said to the king, It was a true report that I heard in mine own land of thy acts and of thy wisdom . . . And behold, the half was not told me (I Kings 10:6,7).

When we read of the Queen of Sheba there immediately arises the question of the historicity of the narrative. Was the Queen of Sheba a real person? The allegation has been made that this story is a myth. In my student days I read a statement by a prominent professor saying, "The Queen of Sheba is a myth. There was no Sheba and there could have been no Queen of Sheba." Many other like statements have been made concerning the Bible. It was said that Moses could not have written the Pentateuch because there was no writing in Moses' day and that Abraham was not an individual but a tribe and the flood was impossible for there were no evidences of the flood. All these statements have been disproved by archaeology. Writing existed at least 1500 years before Moses and tablets from a library in Erech are in the British Museum. The fact of the flood has been fully proved by the University of Pennsylvania expedition in Ur of Chaldee. The greatest living American archaeologist and authority on antiquity W. F. Albright of Johns Hopkins, declared that Abraham was an historic person.

In the year 1950 an expedition was conducted by Mr. Wendell Phillips, President of the American Foundation for the Study of Man, into modern Yemen in Arabia, the site of four ancient kingdoms, Na'in, Hadhramaut, Quatavan and

Sheba. The American Foundation for the Study of Man has directors such as Admiral Nimitz, Lowell Thomas and other outstanding people. The expedition was composed of 15 members who included Professor W. F. Albright of Johns Hopkins, Dr. Charles Inge of Aden, Director of Antiquities, Professor Alexander Honeyman of the Oriental Studies of Scotland's St. Andrews University, Professor Albert Jamme of Oriental Studies at Tunis University and Dr. Friso Heybroek, geologist from The Hague, as well as other prominent scholars. The expedition was conducted in the Wadi Beiham, the site of Timnah, capital of the ancient kingdom and an important city of the period about 1000 B.C. The expedition was equipped with the most modern pushbutton technical material and was conducted under the protection of the British and Sheriff Hussein of modern Yemen. The conclusions of the expedition confirmed in every detail the high civilization, culture, trade and condition which existed in Sheba at the very time the Bible says the Queen came to Solomon.

In addition to this, we have the testimony of Jesus (Luke 11:31). Jesus spoke of the Queen of Sheba as an historical person. Either Jesus was in error or the Queen of Sheba was a real character who had deep desire for a knowledge of the true God and came this long journey to interrogate Solomon, of whose wisdom concerning the name of the Lord she had heard.

A WOMAN WHO WAS INTERESTED IN THE TRUTH

In her own country of Sheba, the Queen had heard the report concerning Solomon. Perhaps we should have a description of this country of Sheba. It was located in the southwestern part of Arabia between the Indian Ocean and the Red Sea. In ancient times, it was called Sabea, then Arabia Felix and today Yemen. It is about as large as Texas and it is noted for its magnificent scenery. Through the center of the area ran a chain of mountains with beautiful and fertile valleys on both sides, irrigated by mountain streams and producing the finest fruits and spices in the world. It was called the region of

Balsamic trees which yielded their gums for spices to be sent to all parts of the wo ld. The citrus fruits included oranges and lemons and in addition were raised fine apricots, world famous Mocca coffee and some of the finest grain. Birds of fair plumage came from far and wide to roost in the cinnamon trees.

Wendell Phillips, of the American Foundation for the Study of Man, said, "The wealth from southern Arabia incense trains supported the economy of four important kingdoms for more than a thousand years. The camel caravans coursed slowly and in great numbers from the incense forest in Hadhramaut, north, through the length of Arabia . . . They returned almost as heavily laden with gold and silver from Egypt, Greece and finally Rome." One can reconstruct in his imagination this picture of green fields, irrigated valleys, forests of trees, fragrant flowers, sweet fruit, wealth from spices and general beauty which marked the area. In the excavation at Timnah statues and inscriptions of a highly cultured order revealed that Timnah existed as a leading city and was destroyed approximately 50 B.C., about 2000 years ago.

The dissemination of information concerning Solomon came to Sheba through commerce. We read that Solomon's own ships went to Tarshish, which is Spain, and to Opher, which probably is India. They brought back peacocks, apes and much gold. Those on their way to India must have passed down the Gulf of Akaba through the Red Sea, into the Indian Ocean. Hence, they went right by the shores of Yemen and it would be very easy for reports of Solomon's wealth, wisdom and way of life resulting from his worship of the true God of heaven to reach the Queen of Sheba (I Kings 10:6).

If we are to take the parallel established by Jesus between the coming of the Queen of Sheba to Solomon and the coming of people unto Him, who was greater than Solomon, then we also have the parallel in the method of dissemination of the truth. You have heard concerning Christ's deity manifested by His pre-existence, His virgin birth, His sinlessness, His teaching, His miracles and His incarnate life. You have heard concerning His life, death on the cross as an atonement for our sins and His resurrection for our justification. You have heard of His ascension to the right hand of the Father, His ministry of intercession, as Mediator between God and man, and His imminent second coming in power and glory to judge the quick and the dead. Hence, you know far more about one greater than Solomon than this Queen of Sheba ever knew about this king of antiquity.

One may easily understand the reluctance of the Queen to believe these things about anybody. She was wealthy, cultured and probably well versed in the knowledge of the day, so that she had a native inability to believe what she heard about Solomon. When these merchants, either from her camel trains or from the passing ships, came to Sheba she summoned them before her presence to testify of the things that they had heard and learned concerning Solomon and his glory. Perhaps you also have found the Gospel incredible when you first heard of it. The news is so wonderful as to be unbelievable. To learn that God loves you, that God Himself came into the world to be your Redeemer, that God died on the cross for you and rose again from the dead to deliver you from sin and death is truly incredible. Yet these facts of the Gospel create in us a desire to hear more, to know firsthand, to investigate for ourselves and not to depend upon the reports of others. Have you had aroused in you a desire for proof for the existence of God, for evidences of the incarnation, for the dependability of the New Testament records, for the credibility of the miracles, for the possibility of prayer which changes things in the world, for assurance concerning your own dead loved ones?

This Queen of Sheba resolved that she would go and see for herself. She was so interested, so disturbed, so curious, so hungry that she determined she would not depend upon the reports of others; she would investigate on her own. This is exactly what Jesus wanted the people of His generation to do; namely, to come to Him, to learn of Him and to be saved by Him. He stood up at the feast and said, "If any man thirst, let him come unto me, and drink. He that believeth on me, as the scripture hath said, out of his belly shall flow rivers of living water" (John 7:37, 38); "I am the light of the world: he that followeth me shall not walk in darkness, but shall have the light of life" (8:12); "I am the way, the truth, and the life: no man cometh unto the Father, but by me" (14:6). As a result, as many as received Him, to them gave He authority to become the sons of God (John 1:12). Such included Matthew, the publican; Mary Magdalene, the demon possessed; Nicodemus, the Pharisee; Joseph of Arimathea, a ruler in Israel; and Zacchaeus, the outcast.

This is the practice which is urged in Scripture. The Bible says, "Come and see"; "O taste and see that the Lord is good"; "Prove me now herewith . . ."; and, "Ye shall seek me, and find me, when ye shall search for me with all your heart." The resolve to see for oneself is a proper resolve.

THE WOMAN INVESTIGATED FOR HERSELF

The Queen of Sheba made her journey to Jerusalem from the uttermost part of the earth. The text says she came "with a very great train, with camels that bare spices, and very much gold, and precious stones." The pomp of this train was very impressive. It was attended by hundreds of guards, by officials of the kingdom, by ladies in waiting, by slaves attending the camels bearing the burdens, by all that was necessary to transport the great wealth she was bringing from her prosperous kingdom. Wendell Phillips said, "The Queen of Sheba's trip to Jerusalem, about 950 B.C., coincided with the greatest expansion of camel caravan trade in ancient history, and it is more than likely that she as head of south Arabia's wealthiest and most powerful state, made the trip to help establish the trade route, as well as to see Solomon." Hers was a long journey. Jesus said, "She came from the uttermost part of the earth." Sheba was between 900 and 1000 miles from Jerusalem as the crow flies, but on foot, through the mountains, valleys and deserts it would be much further and involved a journey of weeks if not months. Yet all this the Queen did seeking to learn from Solomon the ways concerning the name of the Lord. God's promise is that all who make an effort to find God

and the truth will be rewarded by an answer, but these seekers
must be driven by an inner hunger.

Out in Taylor University, Indiana, there is a memorial to
Sammy Morris. Sammy was born in the heart of Africa and
was taken as a slave. He was terribly maltreated and finally he
escaped. He had heard about some missionaries and he made
his way to the mission station. There he was received as one
who worked and ultimately as one who attended school. He
learned to read and write. He learned about the Bible and
with an insatiable hunger he pursued the study of Christian
truth. He wanted to know most of all about the Holy Spirit.
Finally, the missionaries told him all that they knew, but he
still wanted to know more. Then they declared that he would
have to go to New York to meet Stephen Merritt. So Sammy
prayed about this and offered himself to every ship that came
into port. Finally he was signed on as a cabin boy and taken
to New York. Arriving there, he asked to see Stephen Merritt.
In the providence of God, he met someone who knew Stephen
Merritt and he was led to him. Stephen Merritt told him all
that he knew about the Holy Spirit and then sent him out to
Taylor University in Indiana. There he became a great inspiration to the students and to all who knew him until finally he
took sick and died. Literally thousands have been inspired by
the life of Sammy Morris. Sammy was hungry for God and he
sought until he found Him.

When the Queen of Sheba came to Jerusalem to Solomon
we read "she communed with him of all that was in her heart."
Considering this negatively, we may remark that it was not
from curiosity, it was not as a receiver of gifts, and it was not
for matrimony. Her interest was deeper than her curiosity.
She came bringing $3,250,000 in gold as a gift to Solomon, in
addition to invaluable spices and precious stones. She did not
have in mind a political marriage which was so common in
those days. Positively, she came to seek his wisdom and not
his worldly wisdom, but that which begins in the fear of the
Lord. The introduction to the Queen of Sheba declares that
she was interested in "the name of the Lord." She came to

prove Solomon with hard questions because she loved the truth and she sought it in all of its parts. In her we have one who deserves to rank with Socrates in a sincere search for the truth and in his obedience to it. There is nothing wrong in asking questions concerning God and the truth. Remember that the truth is of God and wherever you find the truth you are finding that which belongs to God.

Undoubtedly the word of the approach of this caravan train was given to Solomon and he prepared himself for the arrival of the Queen and her retinue. Upon her arrival she observed all that pertained to Solomon, "the meat of his table, and the sitting of his servants, and the attendance of his ministers, and their apparel, and his cupbearers, and his ascent by which he went up unto the house of the Lord." Solomon's table was served with 30 stall-fed oxen, 200 fat sheep innumerable deer and fowl daily. When I want to give a dinner to a dozen or more of my friends, if I can afford it I get a rib roast. This is quite an indulgence. Imagine what 30 stall-fed oxen per day would mean. Solomon had graced the balustrades of his balconies and the approach of his temple with almug trees which were sandalwood brought from India and when polished were as white as silver. No such almug trees were ever seen again as those which were brought and placed in the temple and palace area of Solomon. Solomon had made the house of the forest of Lebanon in which he had 200 targets of beaten gold around the walls and 300 shields of beaten gold hanging on the walls. He had a temple which, computed according to the requirements of what went into it in addition to the preparations David made before his death, would amount to $2,000,000,000 in our present money. And he had a magnificent palace. Solomon's throne was made of ivory covered with gold. It had six steps on it and on each side of a step was a lion covered with gold and there was not the like of it in any kingdom. Solomon's drinking vessels were all of gold, and silver was nothing accounted of in the days of Solomon. All this the Queen of Sheba observed.

While being entertained by Solomon they conversed of

botany, for Solomon could speak of the "trees, from the cedar tree that is in Lebanon even unto the hyssop that springeth out of the wall." He was well versed in all matters of nature. They spoke of zoology, talked of "beasts, and of fowl, and of creeping things, and of fishes." Solomon was well versed in the things of biology. They talked of geology, for Solomon was an expert in reference to precious stones and metal and expanded the finding of them very widely. In addition, they spoke of the true wisdom which begins in "the fear of the Lord." Solomon told her of the creation of man and of the world. He discoursed upon the stars, calling them by name. He explained to her the fall of man, the promise made to the seed of the woman, the giving of the law, the institution of sacrifice to betoken atonement, the promised Messiah and the establishment of the kingdom of God under the lion of the tribe of Judah.

The conclusion to their conversation was that "there was no more spirit in her." She was convicted of her own insignificance and her ignorance in comparison with Solomon. Here we get a picture of how we feel in the presence of the Lord Jesus Christ. The closer we come to Him, the larger He grows. The more we know about Him, the more there is to know. The more of His truth we apprehend, the more we recognize there is to apprehend and we know our insignificance. The Queen of Sheba was converted. She said, "It was a true report that I heard in mine own land of thy acts and of thy wisdom." It surpassed all that she had heard and she humbled herself in its presence. Who is there who can tell the glory, the beauty, the wealth, the grace, the power and the honor of the Lord Jesus Christ? It is far beyond all reports that we have received. Therefore, the Queen of Sheba made a commitment. She said, "Happy are thy men, happy are these thy servants, which stand continually before thee, and that hear thy wisdom." This was the conclusion of her investigation of Solomon. A similar conclusion should mark an investigation of those of us who come to Jesus Christ. We should be filled with joy and happiness that we can stand in His presence. There is no joy like knowing Him. We could say with the Queen of Sheba, now I know for myself.

A WOMAN WHO INHERITED TRUTH'S BLESSING

The Queen of Sheba received religious truth. She said, "Blessed be the Lord thy God, which delighted in thee, to set thee on the throne of Israel: because the Lord loved Israel for ever." Her contact with Solomon led her thoughts to God. What a testimony this was of Solomon and of his way of discourse with the Queen of Sheba. How this should put us in judgment and condemnation because of our failure to discourse adequately concerning our Lord and Saviour Jesus Christ. She had the concept of God's love and sovereignty in appointing Solomon as king over Israel forever. Can we not see the parallel in the gift of our Lord Jesus Christ to the church forever? Hence, the Queen of Sheba conferred her valuable gifts upon Solomon as the representative of God. She gave him a gift of three and a quarter million dollars in gold, of unparalleled precious spices and of precious stones that had been mined in the mountains of Hadhramaut.

In return, she received of the royal bounty, "King Solomon gave unto the queen of Sheba all her desire" (I Kings 10:13). The desire of the Queen of Sheba as mentioned in this chapter of Scripture was knowledge of the Lord. There is a tradition in Ethiopia that the Emperor of Ethiopia is descended from Solomon by the Queen of Sheba and he bears the title, the Lion of the Tribe of Judah. This is a wresting of this passage of Scripture which is clearly amplified in the context. The Queen of Sheba came desiring to know God and Solomon led her heart to be satisfied in the Lord God. He gave her a full answer to all her questions, "whatsoever she asked." And beside, he gave her many gifts from the royal bounty. Thus we may see that the Lord Jesus Christ is able to answer our questions and God will supply all our needs according to His riches in glory.

This Queen returned the long journey from Jerusalem to Sheba a changed woman who could never again be the same.

She had come in contact with a man who had lifted her thoughts to the Lord and had satisfied the hunger of her heart in the knowledge of God.

Jesus tells us that in Himself a greater than Solomon is here. We have all the information necessary to come to Him and to receive the answers to our questions. Whether we have that answer or not depends upon the response which we make. His encomium is pronounced upon those who come in faith and sincerity.

13

Esther

THE WOMAN WHOSE COURAGE SAVED A NATION

> *And so will I go in unto the king, which is not according to law: and if I perish, I perish* (Esther 4:16).

Esther may well be called a woman who saved a nation. The text which points this up is Esther 4:14 which says, "Who knoweth whether thou art come to the kingdom for such a time as this?" Esther lived in a period of crisis for the Jewish people and God used her as the means of delivering them in this crisis.

It is necessary for us to recognize that western civilization is in a desperate crisis today. Mr. Nikita Khrushchev has said, "We will bury you," and "Your form of society is doomed." As a consistent Marxist, Mr. Khrushchev believes that history has decreed the dissolution of western Christian culture. Mr. Averill Harriman reported after two lengthy interviews with Mr. Khrushchev that he thoroughly believes the West is doomed.

Mr. Frol R. Koslov, the Soviet First Deputy Premier, during his visit to the United States in 1959, declared, "Force will be met with force," if the Berlin dispute reaches the stage of open conflict. The only reason why there is a conflict concerning Berlin at all is because Communists have repudiated their agreement concerning the four-power control of Berlin. If the West abandons free Berlin to the east Germans and thus to the Russians, it will have lost all moral leadership in Europe. In the light of the above statements, it is possible that a small war will be unleashed by the Soviets in Germany in which the eastern Germans, as subject peoples, will fight the cause of the Soviets and Russia will not be embroiled in the war at all. This could easily be a repetition of what has happened in Korea, in Viet-Nam, and what the Communists attempted to do in Formosa.

Since the Communists are dedicated to Marxism, we should ask ourselves what are the basic principles of Marxism. Three should be singled out: First, the principle of godless materialism — namely, that there is nothing in the world except matter. There is no mind, no spirit, no soul, no God but merely the relationship of matter. Thinking is the functioning of a physical brain. The soul is the functioning of the composite man. Since such materialism rules out the existence of God, it also eliminates all such things as absolute morals or ethics and all values derived from the belief in God and in spirit.

The second principle is that man is a material animal with no soul. He is the fruit of the evolutionary process. He is of no value in himself and may be sacrificed upon the altar of social revolution.

Third, is the principle of economic determinism. This principle declares that the economic struggle for bread on the part of mankind is expressed in class struggle which interprets all human relationships. Thus, loyalty, love, sacrifice, heroism and other values are derived from the economic struggle. History has determined or destined that the masses, whether they are called plebes, serfs, or proletarians will ultimately dominate and that government will ultimately be a government of the proletarian class.

The goal of Marxism is world revolution. It seeks to promote revolution through the propaganda and activities of the Communist party in individual nations. When the balance of power has finally been turned in favor of the Communist movement an all-out struggle will be launched to establish the world revolution. Lenin said, "Strike the bourgeoisie as it is necessary. Strike him only in the chest when you are sure of victory."

Thus, the strategy of the Communist movement is to encircle the free nations by Communist nations that have been established by revolution and to incite class war within the free nations through the instrumentality of the Communist party. By this means Communists intend to promote chaos, confusion and conflict. They play upon the conflict of classes, of races and of creeds. They seek to produce degeneracy and corruption until the people are ready for a change, regardless of what that change is. Any activity of the Communists which promotes the revolution is called a peaceful activity. Any activity of the free nations in resisting Communism is called a warlike activity. It is the Communist belief that if they can promote their program, a nation like America can fall like a ripe plum to Communism without warfare.

From the above brief sketch it is evident that the free world stands in great danger of extermination. The warnings, the threats and the actions of the Communists all point toward their seeking to bring about world revolution. Hence, it should be helpful for us to turn to a story of a parallel situation when a people faced extermination but found deliverance. Our deliverance will come through enlightenment, dedication and defense in spiritual depth. Perhaps by studying the conditions in the time of Esther, who was used of God to deliver the Israelites, we may have some principles of guidance.

The Coming to Prominence of Esther

The Book of Esther begins with the demotion of the queen of the Persian empire named Vashti. Persia at this time, approximately 500 B. C., was the world's greatest empire. The Persian king had control over 127 provinces reaching from India to Ethopia. He had chosen as the site of his palace and capital Shushan which was located in an area similar to southern California in climate and beauty. By means of irrigation, the land was a garden of Eden. Flowers of all sorts bloomed, rare birds found refuge in the trees and shrubs, fragrant gardens were attached to the homes, and the palace was a magnificent specimen of architecture with many sections

open to the sky because of the auspicious weather. Here King
Ahasuerus ruled and celebrated his great conquest. The occasion which opens the Book of Esther is a pagan bacchanalian
revel which compromised virtue and decency as it always
does. The king had invited his princes, lords and representatives from the provinces to a great banquet which lasted a full
week. At the end of it, when the king and others were under
the influence of wine and merriment, he commanded Vashti,
the beautiful queen, to appear before them to display her
beauty. Vashti will forever stand as a synonym for purity and
modesty. She had boycotted the feast during the week and
now she refused the king's command. In a Persian court this
meant dire consequences as illustrated by the fact that whoever approached the king without being requested to come
would be put to immediate death. Vashti was removed from
her position as queen of the world's greatest empire and
moved into oblivion. What happened to her we do not know,
but the punishment which she received should be to her
honor. Vashti stands out as a woman of great morality, a
bright light in a heathen background.

It was then that Esther was discovered. We read that
after Vashti had been removed and the king had sobered
down, he remembered his beautiful queen. Then it was that
the suggestion was made that his courtiers search for a new
queen. This meant the bringing in of all the fair virgins
wherever they were found in the empire. Inevitably Esther,
who was a fair, pure and modest maiden, was found and
without her consent was attached to the king's household of
women.

This leads us to ask what kind of a woman Esther was,
since she was catapulted by a Cinderella story, from obscurity to the highest position of that ancient world. First, it is
obvious that she was a peerless beauty. One may admire a
beautiful landscape, or a well-formed horse or animal, or a
strong man, but there is nothing which excites admiration
such as a beautiful woman. Esther was also obedient. She
had been reared by her cousin Mordecai, who had taken her

as an orphan and had treated her as his own daughter (Esther 2:7). The whole narrative reveals that she was obedient to her cousin as she would be to a father. Esther was also humble. Her attitude of leaving her case in the hands of Hegai, the king's chamberlain, and her refusal to request any gift with which to go in to the king, reveals her humility.

On the other hand, a case has been made against Esther. It is said that she hid her nationality during the time that she was in a place of prominence and leadership in the kingdom until this crisis arose. It is often said that she sought to be the queen of a drunken and brutal king. It is alleged that she remained at Shushan when the other Jews had returned to Jerusalem, thus seeking the easy way. And it is declared that she was vengeful in killing her enemies. There is an answer to each of these allegations concerning Esther and we are led to accept the higher view of Esther because she has been given a place in the canon of Scripture which shows that her faith and obedience were acceptable unto God.

The destiny of Esther was to be the saviour of her people. In a parallel way God is looking for men and women whom He may trust today to save His people. The people of God and those committed to righteousness are in desperate need today. There will be a showdown with Communism in the next ten years and God is looking for those who may be used in places of leadership and responsibility.

The Crisis Which Faced Esther and Her People

It was at this time that a plot was hatched by the prime minister of King Ahasuerus to exterminate all the Jews. The provocation came in the action of one Jew, Mordecai who refused to do honor and obeisance unto this prime minister, Haman. Haman was intensely provoked by the action of Mordecai. One cannot help but remember how provoking some of these Jews can be in their aggressiveness. Instead of dealing with Mordecai, Haman extended his hatred to the whole nation. That basic prejudice had existed before this time is evident from other references in Scripture. Individual events were often transferred to the nation and anti-Semitism has been an historical phenomenon across the centuries, both before and after the time of Haman. One thinks of how this was the case with the Jews when they were in Egypt under the dominion of Pharaoh, of how they were made the scapegoats of the National Socialist regime in Germany, and how even today they are being persecuted in Romania by the Communists. Haman determined that he would exterminate the entire race of the Jews.

Without our claiming that the people of the West are the chosen people of God, we do believe that there is a parallel between this conspiracy of Haman to wipe out the Jews, and the present Communist conspiracy to wipe out those who are contaminated with bourgeois philosophy. The Communist theory, based upon materialism, economic determinism, exploitation of the masses, organization of labor, inevitable revolution, the establishment of the dictatorship of the proletariat, the building of state socialism and ultimately the Communist form of society declares that it is inevitable that when the revolution occurs, all those who have been contaminated or infected with bourgeois philosophy must be liquidated. This especially deals with Christians, with leaders of free society and with those who are committed to representative democracy. There is no secret of the intention of the Communists to brutally and ruthlessly liquidate a vast section of present society when the revolution takes place. The difficulty most people have is believing that the Communists mean what they say, and yet every place where the revolution has occurred, they have applied their theory.

This means that Christian civilization stands in very great peril. We must face the possibility of endless small wars, or of even a possible all-out atomic war. We must realize that political warfare will be endless, creating constant tensions which are intended to advance the Communist cause. We must be aware that we are facing a fanatical foe which believes in the superiority of the Marxist and the Socialist viewpoint and of the inevitable victory of that theory and movement. We must recognize that it is possible for a sneak attack to be launched upon our great cities which would wipe out 70% of our population. These possibilities are realities in the crisis in which we presently live.

The Courage Which Wrought Deliverance

This courage in Esther was exemplified by her statement, "If I perish, I perish." She had the courage to seek the favor of the king's scepter, in spite of the law, because of her trust in the providence of God. Esther was aware of her own insecurity. Vashti had already been removed and the law stood upon the Persian books that anyone who approached the king, invading his privacy without invitation, would be put to death. This was an oriental way of dealing with the nuisance of back-door petitioners. Moreover, Esther had not been called into the presence of the king for 30 days. Probably her reputation with the king had been damaged by the innuendo and direct attack of Haman. Hence, she faced the possibility of her own immediate death by breaking the law so as to influence the king on behalf of her people.

Here we should pause to call attention to the hazard which faces anyone who opposes Communism. The first opposition will be in the form of a smear attack upon the character and career of such an individual. Next, there is an attempt to organize opposition so as to remove such a person from a place of leadership. And finally, there is a personal danger to which an individual is exposed by these fanatical people who will stop at nothing to achieve their goal.

Esther had an attitude of dependence upon God. She commanded Mordecai, "Gather together all the Jews . . . and fast ye for me." God is not mentioned in the Book of Esther but His providence and sovereignty are implied in Esther's request for the Jews to fast and her own promise to fast. Such fasting was for the purpose of praying. Here is a good illustration of the power of prayer to change things externally. There are occasions when special providences enter the course of history. Even Arnold Toynbee acknowledges that little things often change the entire course of history. These things must be attributed to divine providence.

In the crisis in which we find ourselves today, God alone can work deliverance from the menace of atheism. Granting this, what folly it is for those of the western nations to repudiate God in action by drunkenness, crime, delinquency, immorality and other sins. What wisdom it would be for us if we would humble ourselves in His presence and seek His face. The Bible tells us that God will not be mocked, that what we sow we shall reap. Israel rebelled against God and God used the brutal and atheistic Assyrians as His army to punish Israel. It may well be that God will again apply this same principle and will use the brutal and atheistic Communist armies of the world to punish the indifferent and careless people of the West.

By Esther's action Israel was saved. The Book of Esther tells us of the diplomacy by which she approached Ahasuerus and implicated Haman in the terrible plot for her destruction and the destruction of her people. She isolated Haman from all others and made him face the accusation alone with the king at a banquet which she had prepared. In the meantime, an event occurred which revealed God's interest and control in the crisis. Ahasuerus could not sleep so he had the chronicles brought to him to be read in order to induce sleep. In this there was read the action of Mordecai in appraising the king of a plot against his life. When the reading was over, the king asked what had been done for Mordecai who had been so loyal to the king. The reply was nothing. Later, when Haman entered the king's presence, he asked him what should be done for the man whom the king delighteth to honor. Haman thought it was himself whom the king was to honor so he declared that he should be clothed in the king's garments, wear the king's crown, ride the king's horse, should be led by the king's most prominent minister throughout the town with the proclamation, "Thus shall it be done to the man whom the king delighteth to honour." Then said the king, "Make haste . . . and do even so to Mordecai the Jew." In this we recognize the control of God over little things which change the course of history, such as the lowering sky and fog which prevented the German air armada from strafing the English fishing ships that evacuated the English army from the coast of Dunkirk and saved England, or such as the storm which smashed the Spanish armada which intended to invade England, or such as the snows of Russia which defeated Napoleon. We cannot help but wonder what purpose God has in permitting the present crisis. Is it one of admonition? Or reproof? Or of judgment?

Through Esther's intercession, Ahasuerus condemned Haman to death and passed the decree that the Jews were permitted to defend themselves on the day on which Haman had decreed their extermination. Thus, the 13th and 14th of Nisan was set aside as a celebration of the Jews which is observed to this day, called the Feast of Purim, to celebrate the deliverance under Esther.

God's sovereign providence superintends events so as to preserve His people and overthrow their enemies. As God did with the Jews under Esther, He is no less able to do for His people this day. Where there is repentance, prayer, godly leadership, the providence of God will be displayed in the deliverance of His people.

14

Elisabeth

The Woman Whose Son Was the Greatest of Men

Among them that are born of women there hath not arisen a greater than John the Baptist; notwithstanding he that is least in the kingdom of God is greater than he (Matt. 11:11).

Greatness is a very indefinite thing. Whether one is great or not depends upon the standard by which he is judged. Individuals may be divided in their opinion of the greatness of a man. It seems, however, that the men of the generation of John the Baptist and those of every generation since have acknowledged that he was great.

The standard of greatness in the case of John is set by God. God knows what is in man; He knows the motives, the thoughts, and the desires of the human heart, and He cannot be mistaken. It was the Son of God who said that "among them that are born of women, there hath not arisen a greater than John the Baptist." John's magnanimous character, his wonderful career, and his flawless courage give him this place as the greatest of those born of women. Without this evaluation by Christ, we probably would not pick John out as the greatest of men. Some of us in looking at Biblical history would decide upon Moses because of his great work of leading the children of Israel out of bondage. Others would decide upon Elijah because he reformed the nation of Israel and preserved the true religion, the worship of Jehovah. Others would decide upon Jeremiah because of his tremendous courage in a time of decadence and because of his great international vision.

Others would even go so far back as the time of Abraham and call the "father of the faithful" the greatest born of women. If we were to evaluate the life of John the Baptist from human standpoints, we would almost say that he was a failure. John left no permanent movement. He left no dynasty. He did not even found a system of thought. Seemingly he died a failure, unaccepted, and a martyr. Yet outside of the kingdom of God, John the Baptist was the greatest of those born of women.

Can it be that John the Baptist surpasses all of the great men of history who were outside the kingdom of God? Think of the military heroes from the time of Leonidas at the Battle of Marathon to Napoleon, including in that long list Alexander, Pompey, Hannibal, Julius Caesar, Genghis Khan, Charlemagne. Here were men who changed the course of nations. They seemed to be the turning-point of history. The biographers of history have called them great. Is it true that John the Baptist, about whom no biography was ever written, is greater than these? Think of the cultural leaders of the earth from the time of Pericles, with the host of outstanding men who were gathered about him during the Golden Age of Greece down to the time of the Victorian Era, and the cluster of great names that were assembled in that period, including all the courts from Constantine to Louis XIV, which came in the interim period. Was John the Baptist greater than the men who were the centers around which these cultural periods revolved? Think again of the philosophers from the time of Thales to Immanuel Kant, including Plato, Aristotle, Philo, Plotinus, Anselm, Aquinas, Occam, Locke, Descartes, Spinoza, and Hume. Great as were all of these personages, none can compare with the son of the woman about whom we speak, that is, on the plane of divine judgment. He excelled them all.

Wherever we find a great man in history, his greatness will be largely due to the greatness of a mother who went before him. In the Granary Burying Ground, next to our church, there is a monument to the mother and father of Benjamin Franklin, a woman who had thirteen children and who trained them in the fear of God and in the honor of thrift. Who can say that the greatness of Benjamin Franklin was not due to his mother? Once when the mother of George Washington was told of the promise of little George, she said, "George is a good boy." She had inculcated in him the sense of loyalty, of humility, and of value that caused him to choose between a road of ease and one of sacrifice for the sake of his country. Even Abraham Lincoln said, "All that I am I owe to my mother." Whenever God wished to produce a man who would be great in His eyes, He always prepared a mother first. That is why in so many cases the great men of the world have been children of old age. The women have been prepared through years of waiting, of prayer, and of meditation until ultimately God gave them the desire of their hearts. Witness the case of the aged Sarah and the birth of Isaac, of Rachel and the birth of Joseph, of the wife of Manoah and the birth of Samson, of Hannah and the birth of Samuel, and of Elisabeth and the birth of John.

This woman Elisabeth was a true daughter of Aaron in the time of Caiaphas, which designated a very degenerate period. Sholem Asch, in his book, *The Nazarene*, is very accurate in his description of the hatred with which Caiaphas was held by the people because of the wickedness of the high priesthood and also of his exploitation of the masses of the people. Caiaphas set the standard for many of the lesser priests, but this daughter of Aaron was one of true piety and of devout heart. She was a woman who had long prayed for a child but who had been denied the desire of her heart. Thus she was under a reproach in Israel because she was childless. Elisabeth was one whose life was bound up in the Lord's work. She believed all the prophecies about the Messiah and also about the forerunner of the Messiah, who would first come before the advent of the Son of God. Like the devout mothers of Israel, she longed that she might have a child and that that child should at least be the forerunner, if not the Messiah Himself. Yet as the years passed, the hopelessness of the dream bore itself in upon her, and she devoted herself utterly to the Lord's work and to that alone.

When John came, however, Elisabeth communicated to

her child all of her hopes and dreams and aspirations. She poured her own life into him through training and teaching until he knew the Scriptures and the great hopes as well as she herself. Not only did this child have an annunciation in a supernatural way concerning his future, but Elisabeth fulfilled every instruction that was given to her and every requirement concerning one who might be the forerunner of the King. Because of what Elisabeth did, which enabled her son to become the greatest of men, she stands supreme among the mothers of history with the exception, of course, of the mother of our Lord. In our consideration of this woman, we invite your attention to three topics: first, Elisabeth and Mary; second, Elisabeth and John; third, Elisabeth and Jesus.

I. Elisabeth and Mary

The birth narratives of John the Baptist and of Jesus are closely intertwined in the Scripture so that no separation between them is possible. It is necessary when we are talking about one of them to talk also about the other. This interconnection is found in the story included in the first chapter of Luke's Gospel.

The father of John the Baptist was Zacharias, a priest, who served his course in the Temple, performing the daily sacrifice of incense on the golden altar before the veil. He was a godly man, who walked blameless according to the law, who fulfilled his duty, and whose practice was the incarnation of the requirements of the Mosaic Law. To this man, Almighty God sent the angel Gabriel, who appeared to him while he was burning incense and offering prayer upon the altar at the evening hour of sacrifice. Zacharias was greatly troubled but received this reply, "Fear not, Zacharias: for thy prayer is heard; and thy wife Elisabeth shall bear thee a son, and thou shalt call his name John" (Luke 1:13). This greatest of all angels then proceeded to inform Zacharias of the greatness of the child in the sight of the Lord, of the manner of his life and of the ministry which he should perform. Said he, "He shall go before Him in the spirit and power of Elias, to turn the hearts of the fathers to the children, and the disobedient to the wisdom of the just; to make ready a people prepared for the Lord." Zacharias then responded, "Whereby shall I know this? for I am an old man, and my wife well stricken in years." This was doubt on the part of Zacharias and because of it Gabriel commanded that he should be dumb until the word was fulfilled. This judgment on Zacharias was a sign to both him and to his wife that the Lord would perform His Word. As soon as Zacharias' course was finished, he returned to his home in the hill country of Judah and remained there until the birth of John the Baptist.

One might very well use his historical imagination to know what occurred in the house of Zacharias and Elisabeth in the days preceding the birth of John the Baptist. With the full knowledge of the annunciation, and with the proof in the coming of Mary, who had also seen the angel Gabriel, these devout parents must have turned to the Old Testament Scriptures and read and reread the prophecies both of the Messiah and of His forerunner, treasuring them in their hearts. Then came the day when the happy event of John's birth occurred. Within a week, all the relatives gathered together for the service of circumcision and naming the child. They insisted that he should be called Zacharias after his father, but Elisabeth clung to the name "John." Therefore, they decided that the father would settle the matter and they asked him. He, taking a tablet, wrote the name, "John," which means "the grace of God." Immediately the lips and tongue of Zacharias were opened and he spoke in the words of a poem which he composed during the time of his dumbness, celebrating the wonders of God and of the child who was now born. This is called "The Benedictus"; it emphasizes the fact that God has visited and redeemed His people and raised up a horn of salvation for them to give the remission of sins through the tender mercy of God. "The Dayspring from on high hath visited us, to give light to them that sit in darkness and in the shadow of death, to guide our feet into the way of peace" (Luke 1:78, 79). This aged couple knew, and many of their friends in the hill country of Judea knew, that God had begun the redemptive process.

The faith of Elisabeth was demonstrated in this series of events. First, we have the joy with which she received the glad tidings from Zacharias that the angel of God had visited him and announced the birth of a son. There is no record of the fact that she doubted the angel's word. Rather it immediately came to pass according to the word of the angel in her life. Within five months, Mary visited at her home in Judah, and as her cousin came into her presence, both women bearing these two wonderful sons, she greeted her with an outburst of song inspired by the Holy Ghost, saying "Blessed art thou among women, and blessed is the fruit of thy womb. And whence is this to me, that the mother of my Lord should come to me? . . . for there shall be a performance of those things which were told her of the Lord" (Luke 1:42, 43, 45). There was no jealousy in Elisabeth's nature. She did not wonder why the Lord did not send the Messiah instead of the forerunner through her, why she was not chosen instead of Mary. Instead she pronounced the blessedness of Mary, exalted her, and strengthened her faith by her own confidence in the fulfillment of the divine promise. What a source of joy and strength and of blessing these two women were to each other during these three months in their lives can well be imagined! Moreover, Elisabeth was very faithful to the orders she had received from the angel through Zacharias concerning John's name, concerning the environment and training he should receive as a child, and concerning his teaching. He was dedicated to the Lord as a Nazarite. He should not touch strong drink and, like Samson, I suppose that a razor did not come upon his head. He was separated unto the Lord from the time of his birth, and he was filled with the Holy Ghost from before his birth, in all of which things we see the faith of Elisabeth in the infinite God.

The early life of John the Baptist was under the leadership and guidance of Elisabeth. He lived in that simple home in the hill country of Judah. Though Zacharias was probably away at Jerusalem at times in the performance of his duties as priest, nevertheless Elisabeth carried on the work in the home, bearing the responsibility of training this wonderful child. Happy childhood days mean more in one's life than almost anything else, and what days John must have spent in this godly family as they read to him the Torah, as they prayed together, and as they instructed him in the greatness of the task that was before him. Undoubtedly the later preaching of John was all due to the teaching of these parents. We read that the boy was filled with the Spirit from his birth and that he waxed strong in spirit (Luke 1:80). Under the tutelage of his mother he grew in the Spirit. There was an enlargement of his soul. Though he was filled with the Spirit from birth, nevertheless as he grew in manhood, his capacity for the Spirit was enlarged. Then he was in the desert until the day of his showing unto Israel. What a renunciation this must have been on the part of his mother, to allow him to leave and go into the desert for fasting and prayer and meditation, to live the life of a Nazarîte! There, with special food of honey and wild locusts, with the pure air and the strong sunshine, his brown, clean body developed with his mind. There the Spirit who was within him permitted him to commune with God, and there the message instilled by his own mother and announced by the angel was developed under the guidance of God. John was sent from his mother's care to do the will of God regardless of what that should cost.

II. Elisabeth and John

Just as when Jacob was an old man and had been separated long from his beloved wife Rachel, he looked at Joseph and Benjamin and in them saw the image of his much loved wife; just so whenever God looked upon John the Baptist He must have seen Elisabeth, the devout, sanctified woman of Israel. When John was in the forefront of the Christian ministry, Elisabeth was there with him. Thus it was that Susannah Wesley stood in thousands of churches in England and Nancy

Hanks Lincoln was in the White House of the United States, not personally, but represented in their sons.

The ministry of John the Baptist began with his showing unto Israel as the preparatory servant of the Lord. First, there was his message, which was given to the multitudes who came. He preached "Repent, for the kingdom of heaven it as hand." In that message of repentance, he told them to bring forth fruits meet for repentance because the judgment of God was impending. He said to the publican, "Exact no more than that which is appointed you;" to the soldier, "Do violence to no man, neither accuse any falsely, and be content with your wages;" to the people, "He that hath two coats, let him impart and give to him that hath none;" to the Pharisees, "The axe is laid to the root of the tree, and every tree which bringeth forth not good fruit is hewn down and cast into the fire" (Luke 3:1-14). Though he had spoken much of repentance and of judgment, he also spoke much of mercy and forgiveness. His message was, "Behold the Lamb of God, who taketh away the sin of the world" (John 1:29). This message is the heart of Christianity, the message of the cross, the message of Calvary, the message of Easter, the message of redemption. John saw his successor, the Lord Jesus, as the Saviour of the world. He proclaimed the Messiah, for he said, "There cometh one mightier than I after me, the latchet of whose shoes I am not worthy to unloose. He shall baptize you with the Holy Ghost and with fire" (Luke 3:16). John acknowledged that the person of Christ was utterly without sin, for he said, "I have need to be baptized of you, and comest Thou to me?" (Matt. 3:14.) He recognized also that his great work was to be that of the King of a spiritual kingdom. This mighty message to the people aroused enthusiasm and faith on the part of the multitude. They were ready to prepare themselves for the coming of the Messiah. When the religious leaders came to John and examined his message and questioned him as to whether he was the Messiah, whether he was Elias, or whether he was Jeremias, or on what authority he performed his baptism, John gave them a scathing message, calling them a "generation of vipers," telling them that God would cast them off and raise up children of stones to Abraham. He seemed to sense that these Sadducees and Pharisees would reject the Lord Jesus Christ and in anticipation he spoke the message of judgment. Then, to Herod, the chief ruler of the land, John fearlessly gave a message of correction and criticism. He told him that it was not lawful for him to take as wife the woman of his own brother (Matt. 14:1-12). He denounced this as a great sin against the moral and spiritual law. Thereby he incurred the wrath of Herod and also of Herodias, which was ultimately to cause his own death. In this mighty ministry to the multitude, to the ecclesiastical, religious people and also to the civil powers, John revealed something of his greatness.

John was also great in personal faith, and this personal faith had been inspired in him through his own mother's knowledge of the Lord. His mother told him that the Messiah would be born shortly after him, that he was to prepare the hearts of the people by preaching repentance and turning them unto God; but John did not know when the Messiah would appear. All he knew was that God had given him a sign that when he saw the Holy Spirit descend upon a man in the form of a dove, that was the Lord. Hence, when John was baptizing the Lord Jesus Christ and the heavens opened and the dove descended (or at least the Spirit descended as a dove), and when a voice was heard, "This is my beloved Son in whom I am well pleased," John knew that this Man Jesus was the Son of God (Matt. 3:16, 17). John had already professed his faith in Him because he could see that he had need to be baptized of Christ. Later, John was willing to deny himself utterly for the Lord Jesus Christ, for when men came to him and said, "Rabbi, He whom thou baptized beyond Jordan now baptizeth and all men go to Him," he said, "Did I not say unto you that a man can receive nothing unless he be given it from above? . . . I am not the Christ but I am sent before Him . . . He must increase but I must decrease"(John 3:25-30). Here John revealed his willingness to set aside himself to exalt the Lord Jesus Christ. Though it would mean his death, though it would mean the end of his ministry, the loss of his great audience, he was willing to do all for the Lord Jesus Christ. Finally, when he was apprehended and put in prison because of his courage, and the doubt began to enter into his soul, he sent two of his disciples unto the Lord Jesus to ask, "Art Thou He who should come, or look we for another?" (Matt. 11:2, 3.) In that sentence we can behold all of the sorrow, the loneliness, the heartaches, the disappointment, the disillusionment, and the doubt of John's soul, for his revelation was imperfect. He knew not the kind of kingdom that the Lord Jesus was to establish, and when he did not see an earthly kingdom set up and himself liberated from prison, he began to doubt. The response the Lord Jesus gave to John is one that ought to reassure us all as to the nature of Christ's kingdom. He said, "Go and show John those things which ye do hear and see: the blind receive their sight, and the lame walk, the lepers are cleansed, and the deaf hear, the dead are raised up, and the poor have the gospel preached unto them, and blessed is he whosoever shall not be offended in Me" (Matt. 11:4-6). Whatever faith John had at his death must have been reassured and strengthened by this statement of Christ.

John's greatness was also revealed in the powerful influence he exercised. First, that influence was revealed on Herod. Later, when Christ was teaching and was performing miracles and the multitudes assembled to Him, Herod said, "It is John the Baptist who has risen from the dead" (Matt. 14:1, 2). Herod had beheaded John but believed that death could not hold him. His influence was also exerted on Jesus, for Jesus said concerning John, "What went ye forth into the wilderness for to see? A reed shaken with the wind? But what went ye out for to see? A man clothed in soft raiment? Behold, they that wear soft raiment are in king's houses. But what went ye forth for to see? A prophet? Yea, I say unto you, and more than a prophet, for this is he of whom it is written. Behold I send My messenger before My face which shall prepare My way before thee. Verily I say unto you, among them that are born of women, there hath not arisen a greater than John the

Baptist" (Matt. 11:7-11). Jesus forever placed John upon that pinnacle of greatness to which none other could ever come. Moreover, the people acknowledged John also as great, for when the Lord Jesus was in controversy with the Pharisees, He put the question to them, "The baptism of John, whence was it, from heaven or of men?" and they could not answer Him, because if they said, "From heaven," then their guilt would have been evident in not accepting him, and if they said, "From men," they feared the people, because all the people accepted John as a great prophet (Luke 20: 4-7). Here then we have Elisabeth living again in her son John, in great influence over the people, in great faith, and in great works before men.

III. ELISABETH AND JESUS

We have just quoted the words of Jesus in which He said, "Among all them that are born of women, there hath not arisen a greater than John the Baptist." Here we have the emphasis of Christ upon the part of woman in John's greatness. The Lord acknowledged that Elisabeth was partly responsible for the greatness of this son John, just as any mother is responsible for the greatness of her own son, but the Lord Jesus did not stop here. He said, "Notwithstanding he that is least in the kingdom of heaven is greater than he." In this we receive a teaching applicable to every mother who brings a son into the world.

The question arises: What then has the least believer now that John the Baptist did not have? The difference lies in the difference between the age of the law and that of grace, which were separated by the cross of Christ. The best that John or any of his age or any of those who preceded him could do was to hope for the promises of God. All believers, including Abraham, David, Solomon, Hezekiah, and Josiah, and the prophets, awaited Christ's coming and looked diligently into the promises to understand what manner of salvation this was that God had foretold; and yet they could not fully understand. The saints of old, including John the Baptist, were resting upon the promises. Blessed as they were, they could not say, "My sins are blotted out. My iniquities are all gone." Before the death and resurrection of Christ, they could only look forward and say, "It shall be blessed indeed." They could be sure that it was God's intention, but they did not know it as an accomplished fact. They still had to come to God through the sacrifices of the priesthood, through the mediatorship of others. They could not come to Him directly as priests themselves into the presence of those things that were typified by the tabernacle and the law and the sacrifice. John was able to announce that the kingdom was at hand, but John could not enter that kingdom. In John's day, the greatest in the sight of God could not enjoy the privileges of the least who were in the kingdom of God.

The kingdom means that reconciliation has been accomplished and that believers are in Christ, that they are born again, forgiven of their sin, justified in the presence of God, and accepted as righteous in His sight. Believers today are priests unto God. An inestimable value was set by God upon the death of Christ upon the cross, and because of that death He can accept sinful men in the beloved as His sons and as righteous in His sight. Now, because everything is done, God can invite souls not to forget their sin, not to turn away their eyes from them, but looking at them fairly and fully before the cross of Christ, He calls upon them to say, "The blood of Jesus Christ, His Son, cleanseth us from all sin" (I John 1:6). Knowing this, the priesthood today is not only superfluous but it is evil, for it separates the soul from God. Every believer is a priest now. It is the believer's God-given privilege to draw near to the holiest of all, with sin judged and his iniquities purged away, so that he may be thoroughly happy in the presence of God while he is still on earth.

This is not a promise — but it is a fact. The difference between a promise and an experience is the difference of being in prison with the promise that you will be brought out and the fact of your liberty when you are brought out. The difference is the difference between being in prison and having liberty. Thus the difference between John and the believer is the difference between having sin upon one, knowing that it will be forgiven, and the knowledge of having one's sin taken away through the cross of Christ.

The kingdom, then, means that one has complete assurance that, because of the death of Christ, he is free from all sin. He is able to take his place in the sight of God exactly where Christ is. God gives us Christ's own standing in His sight. Through the ministry of the Holy Ghost who is now in the believer the child of God is able to draw near unto the Father in the name of Christ, clothed in the nature of Christ, holding Christ's own standing before God, and thus able to ask God in the name of Christ for those things that are for the glory of Christ. This privilege is far beyond anything that could ever have been had or understood under the law. Thus, though John was the greatest of all in the Old Testament dispensation, the greatest of all outside the kingdom of God, yet the least Christian, the least believer, mediated by the death of Christ in his relationship with God, is greater than John the Baptist.

Whenever, then, a child is brought into the kingdom of God, both that child and he who brings him into the kingdom take a place greater than Elisabeth's and John the Baptist's. Elisabeth's son was the greatest of men, but the son of any spiritual believer, in faith, may be greater than he. What a privilege then it is to be a mother in Israel of spiritual children, born through the travail of soul in prayer, born into the kingdom of God. The privileges of the kingdom of God are available for all now. We do not have to say, "Repent," as did John, "for the kingdom of God is at hand." We may say, "Repent and believe for the kingdom of God is here. The kingdom of God is yours for the taking. You should cry unto God that you might be acceptable unto Him as a child of the kingdom." And just as the dispensation that John announced came, so also that dispensation will come to its end, and with the end of this dispensation of grace, we shall have the end of the opportunity of being one of the world's greatest people, greater than Abraham,

Isaac, Jacob, David, or John the Baptist, for surely the destiny of the church, according to the Scripture, will be higher and greater than that of any of the saved in all of the ages of the world's history.

Hence we hold out the promise to any man today that, though John the Baptist was great in character and in courage and in career, you may be greater than John in character because you are redeemed, in privilege, because of your standing in Christ, and in destiny because you will belong to the bride of Christ. The way to seal these privileges is to come to God by repentance, by faith, by trust in the Saviour now, that you may be sealed through the gift of the Holy Ghost. Remember, "among those born of women there hath not arisen a greater than John the Baptist; notwithstanding the least in the kingdom of God is greater than he."

15

Mary

The Noblest Woman of All

> *A sword shall pierce through thine own soul also* (Luke 2:38).

Mary richly deserves her high place of exaltation among women. Mary is called in the Bible, "The mother of our Lord." This does not entitle her to worship nor does it give sanction to all the legends about the person of Mary, but it should cause us to give to her honor and praise and exaltation, which is her due. Because two branches of the Christian church have unduly exalted Mary to the position of deity, we who cling to the Bible teaching are not to go to the other extreme of depreciating Mary. Some of the early fathers, such as Tertullian, Origen, and Chrysostom, did this very thing. Mary deserves an exceedingly high place, and we have no right to deny it to her. Certainly whatever could be attained to or exercised by any woman must have been Mary's status before she was graciously chosen by God to be overshadowed by the Holy Ghost and to become the mother of the Lord Jesus Christ.

For many centuries the Roman Catholic Church believed that Mary's conception was also miraculous, but in 1854 it pronounced the dogma of the immaculate conception. This dogma states that Mary's person was not cursed by original sin and that she came into this world different from any other man or woman who bears the responsibility of original guilt and pollution. Mary was given a unique place in the human race. This dogma is based upon the text in Luke, "Blessed

171

art thou among women." It is true that the Bible calls Mary "highly favored," "blessed among women," and designates her as an object of divine grace, but it never puts her in the unique catagory that is given to her by Roman Catholicism. The main fact that invalidates this teaching is that if it was possible for Mary to be born without sin and to remain sinless throughout her entire life because of a special enduement of the grace of God, then there would have been no necessity for the coming of a Saviour. The one and only Person who lived without sin was the Lord Jesus Christ. Roman Catholicism teaches that Mary was assumed into heaven or taken up into heaven without death. About this the Bible certainly has nothing to say, and the only evidence is that of a late tradition that arose because no one knows where Mary was buried, and because it was a revolting thought to men that the body of Mary, out of which was taken the body of the Lord Jesus Christ, should be subject unto corruption.

There can be no doubt, however, that Mary was a special object of the grace of God. Her choice was an act of election on the part of the Lord. Mary was highly favored because she was the recipient of this divine selection and grace. She was to be the closest to the Son of God during His earthly life and was to share His filial affection during His years in the Nazareth home. Mary's reply to the angel, "Be it unto me according to thy word," reveals that she was a woman of faith. She accepted the announcement of God to her concerning this great wonder of a virgin birth and the coming of the Son of God. Hence, when Elisabeth greeted her, she said, "Blessed is she that believed, for there shall be a performance of those things which were told her from the Lord." We acknowledge that Mary's faith was a gift from almighty God and there was no merit in it, but from the very beginning, Mary believed.

Many were the women from the beginning of creation, when Eve received the protoevangelium, who had hoped that they might be the mother of the Messiah. This was the hope of Sarah, again of Hannah, again of Elisabeth, and of others throughout the centuries, but God looked down on the human race and chose the one lone, demure Jewish maiden from the town of Nazareth, and we ask why. The answer can only be, if we exclude the sovereign grace of God, that God looks upon the heart. In looking upon the heart of Mary, what did He see? The record concerning her suggests to us that He saw first, *A Pure Heart;* second, He saw *A Pondering, Meditative Heart;* and third, He saw *A Pierced Heart of Sympathetic Suffering.*

I. The Pure Heart of This Noble Woman

Sacred art traditionally depicts the angel of the annunciation presenting Mary with a branch of a lily as an emblem of her purity. Well may we consider her as such. Either one of two alternatives must be taken concerning Mary. She is the purest and the highest of women or else Mary must be considered a common harlot. Even to suggest the latter is to raise indignation in the heart of a true Christian, and yet that is the suggestion made by every preacher and every teacher who denies the Virgin Birth of our Lord. In the third century A.D., when Origen was refuting the charges brought by a heathen, Celcus, against the Christians, he spoke of the allegation by Celcus that Jesus was born of Mary and a Roman soldier, by name Ponthera. This simply means that He was born out of wedlock and was illegitimate. It is a rather crass thing to make such a statement concerning one who has taken such a high place in the minds of millions of people throughout the world, but the same statement is made in a refined way whenever one teaches that Jesus was not born as the Bible says He was born. If the Lord Jesus Christ was not Joseph's son, and if he was born not of the unique, creative power of God, then He was an illegitimate son of Mary. Thus you see that you must either accept the Bible and Christian teaching about the noble life of Mary or you must repudiate both her and the Lord Jesus Christ.

If we accept the purity of Mary, then we have the great Christian doctrine of a Virgin Birth. When it became known to Joseph that Mary was with child, he contemplated putting her away, not publicly, but privately. We may be well assured that there must have been a very heartbreaking scene between these two lowly lovers of Nazareth, Joseph kindly but firmly making an accusation and wrongfully deciding that he could never have Mary as his wife, hurt though this terrible fact did. We may assume that it was on account of this that Mary took her trip to Elisabeth in the hill country of Judah. With what a heavy heart and a fearful soul she must have traversed those hills and vales on the long road leading down through Samaria, past the well of Sychar, through Jerusalem, over the Mount of Olives and on to Bethlehem, and then into the mountains of Judah. Her heart was heavy because of Joseph's action. Her fears were keen because of the shame which would come to her in the world, and yet there was always the reassuring message of the angel that had been given to her and the confidence of her faith that the God who now was fulfilling His prophecies would care also for her. This gives some conception of what it must have meant to Mary to have these days of fellowship, of communion, and of personal comfort in the presence of her cousin Elisabeth, who also had received a message from the angel, which message confirmed that which was given to Mary, the ever present evidence of which was the dumb Zacharias sitting under his fig tree or going about the house.

The Virgin Birth as taught in the Bible will ever remain a fundamental doctrine of the church. This is not only because it is a sign but because it is essential to the being of the Saviour. Eight centuries before, the prophet had said, "This shall be a sign unto you. A virgin shall conceive and bear a Son, and shall call His name Immanuel" (Isa. 7:14). This prophecy to the Davidic house and to the women of Israel accounts for the immediate acceptance by Mary of the angelic announcement and also by Joseph of the angel's command. The expectation of a Virgin Birth was in the Hebrew Scriptures. When it actually occurred it was inscripturated as a fact in the narratives of Matthew and of Luke. There is no possible way by which the Virgin Birth may be deleted from these narratives. The Virgin Birth was early accepted by the church, and it has always been accepted. The Apostolic Fathers, the Apologists, and the Fathers of the church all believed in the Virgin Birth, as their own statements testify.

It is true that as early as the time of Justin Martyr, namely, 150 A.D., it was spoken against, but Simeon had said that this Child should be a sign spoken against, and of all the doctrines in the Bible probably this one has been singled out for more ridicule and more opposition than any other. It has been said that it was derived from paganism and that because Jesus was a great personality, men decided that He must have been descended from a god, as Persis or Plato or Alexander were declared to be descended from heathen deities. Men have pointed out the differences in the genealogies, and that both of them claim that Jesus was descended from Joseph rather than Mary. They have argued the impossibility of a Virgin Birth and also have declared that since the rest of the Bible is silent upon this subject, it could not have taken place, but all such arguments overlook the fact that the Virgin Birth was an absolute essential to the Person of Christ as the Son of God. Without this teaching we have a human Jesus, we have a sinful Mary, and we have a fallible Bible. With this doctrine as the basis of our faith, we have a Christ who is Immanuel, that is, "God with us."

The meaning of the Virgin Birth is that God is with us, that the Incarnation has taken place, and that once in time the eternal Deity became flesh and dwelt among us, that He suffered as we suffer, that He died and rose again. Quite truly we may see that this Child of Mary was God. The whole composite picture proves this — the picture of His miracles, of His sinlessness, of His teaching, of His death upon the cross, and of His resurrection from the dead. He likewise claimed to be God. He claimed to have the authority to speak for God, and He declared that He was equal with the Father. Had Jesus been born of any earthly father, there is no sense in which He could actually have been what He claimed to be and what His life declared Him to be. On the other hand, Jesus was as truly a man as He was God. He received Mary's flesh and blood, and He was subject to temptations and trials and sorrows just as any other man. In fact, He was the perfect representative of all mankind.

In Christ, thus, there were two natures in one Person, the nature of God and the nature of man. Well has this been pointed out by one Bible teacher in reference to the first promise concerning the Messiah. It says in Genesis that the seed of the woman should bruise the head of the serpent. Now it is obvious to all that a woman does not have seed, but is like the earth. She receives the seed, which when planted grows and bears fruit in life. Thus in the very first promise given in the garden of Eden, we have the implication of a Virgin Birth, for it does not say the seed of the man, but the seed of a woman, which would be absurd and a manifest impossibility were it not by the direct creative power of God. This God-man is Immanuel, or "God with us," the Saviour. He is the fleshly representative of true humanity, and He is a real representative of true Deity through the Holy Ghost, such a Being that God could place upon Him the tremendous value which He did in order to bring about the atonement and the satisfaction of divine law for the human race. Thus we say that the Incarnation was the only way. Accept the purity of Mary, and you must go on to the great doctrine of the Incarnation. Or, if you accept the doctrine of the coming of God into the world in the form of the human Jesus, then you must accept the doctrine of Mary's purity and of the Virgin Birth.

II.   The Pondering Heart of This Noble Woman

If there is any clue to the reason Mary was chosen by God to become the mother of the Lord, it would be contained in the statement, "She pondered all these things in her heart" (Luke 2:19). Such pondering followed the salutation of the angel, the prophecy of Simeon, and the sayings of the boy Jesus. It reveals a meditative, devout, modest, reticent, worshipful, Jewish maiden, who was the example of all that is best in woman. We hold that Mary symbolizes all that is good and pure and beautiful in motherhood.

Perhaps Mary had more about which to ponder in connection with the birth of her Son than other mothers have in connection with the birth of their children, but there is sufficient of the mysterious, the supernatural, and the wonderful in the life of any child to cause a mother's heart to ponder over whence that life came, where it would go, and what it would be while it was here upon earth. How often as we look into the life of a little child being presented for Christian baptism, we wonder what will be the future for that life. Will it be hardship and shame or will it be honor and fame?

Thus it was no doubt that Mary presented her Child in the Temple and looked into the dim future to ascertain the meaning of the angelic annunciation concerning this life. The wondrous light which had appeared unto her and out of which came the angel Gabriel while she had prayed and read her Scriptures, lingered long over her life. In response to her question, "How shall this be?" those words, "The Holy Ghost shall come upon thee, and the power of the Highest shall overshadow thee: therefore also that holy thing that shall be born of thee shall be called the Son of God . . . for with God nothing is impossible," contained such a depth of meaning that, ponder as she would, Mary could not ascertain the fulness thereof. Who has done more than that today concerning the doctrine of the kenosis or the emptying of Himself and the taking upon Himself of human flesh by Christ? We cannot criticize this Jewish maiden for lack of understanding.

Mary must also have pondered in her heart the salutation of Elisabeth when she said, "Blessed art thou among women, and blessed is the fruit of thy womb. And whence is this to me, that the mother of my Lord should come to me?" Here again were words that designated her Child as the Messiah. How Mary must have pondered when the shepherds came to the Bethlehem manger and related that they had seen angels and heard an annunciation, saying, "Glory to God in the highest, and on earth peace, good will among men." Again, when the wise men came presenting their gold and their frankincense and myrrh, saying that they had seen a star in the east which signified, according to their knowledge, that the Christ, the King of the Jews, was born. Then, finally, how she must have pondered as she presented this wonderful Babe in the Temple and heard Simeon say, "Lord, now lettest Thou Thy servant depart in peace, according to Thy Word: for mine eyes have seen Thy salvation, which Thou hast prepared before the face of all people." Again and again throughout Mary's life she pondered and repondered these events which had come to her, that, like the prophets, she might know how the Spirit which was in her did signify that these things should come to pass.

Mary's was a high state of faith, for she believed, due to her meditations upon the Lord Jesus Christ. She believed what the angel said about Him and thus was convinced that this was to be a Virgin Birth and her Son was to be the Son of God. She did not declare this unto others, but kept it in her own heart, quietly meditating upon its meaning. Moreover, Mary believed from the very beginning in the Messiahship of her Son, with all that the Scriptures promised to be fulfilled through Him. She may have wondered why the kingdom was not established, why all the Old Testament prophecies about that kingdom were not fulfilled if her Son were the King, and yet, in spite of it all, she commanded the servants of the house at Cana of Galilee, saying, "Whatsoever He saith unto you, do it" (John 2:5). Mary knew that when Jesus undertook to solve a problem, it was always solved. There the lack of wine was corrected by His turning the water into wine, an act of omnipotence. Yes, Mary believed in her own Son because she had pondered much upon Him.

One's belief and one's thoughts always lead to one's actions. Thus it was that obedience marked the life of Mary. She obeyed the Holy Spirit in the annunciation by the angel, saying, "Be it unto me according to thy word." She obeyed the Lord Jesus Christ when He commanded her to now be subject unto John, His beloved disciple. Mary also was very understanding of the Lord Jesus Christ. Even in the days when she did not know what it meant when He said, "Wist ye not that I must be about My Father's business?" she did not seem to question deeper but waited until He should tell her more. She also persevered in her faith. Even during the time of the waning of Jesus' popularity, during His trial, His scourging, and His crucifixion, she remained with Him to the end. When others called Him a malefactor and ridiculed Him, Mary stood at His cross, blessing Him and weeping for Him. Mary was even true to her Son and to His disciples after His death, for she remained with them in the Upper Room, praying for ten days for the coming of the Holy Ghost. She was the recipient along with the apostles of this great blessing. It is true that Mary is not given any prominent place thereafter in the whole of the Scriptures, nor is she even referred to in the Acts or in the Epistles, except at this time at Pentecost, but we may be sure that as Mary's life wore on she did not lose the attribute of pondering over events that had occurred to her earlier.

III. The Pierced Heart of This Noble Woman

Simeon had said to her, when she presented the Lord in the Temple, "A sword shall pierce through thine own soul also" (Luke 2:35). On the cross, we read, "One of the soldiers with a spear pierced His side, and forthwith there came out blood and water." We know that the heart of Christ was truly pierced by a spear. Was Mary's also pierced, and if so, how? Is it not strange that whoever comes near to Jesus Christ has always to drink some cup of sorrow or to have a pierced heart? Think of how Mary's heart was pierced and of how Joseph's soul was pierced by a sword. Each of the disciples was also made to drink the cup of woe, and that cup of suffering exists for believers unto this day.

We may be sure that when Jesus' heart was pierced, Mary's was also, because of her complete identification with Him in life. Hers was the parent-child relationship, that which is blood of my blood, bone of my bone, the closest possible in life. Mary had suffered in the birth of Christ. She had suffered during His life, and she suffered in His death. Mary so believed in Christ that she was one of His disciples, doing the things He was bidding His followers. Mary, as she stood by the cross of Christ suffering with Him, is an example of all who are crucified with Christ by faith, those who take up their cross and follow Him. Paul said that He made up in his body the sufferings that were lacking in the body of Christ, and there is a real sense in which that must be done by us all. This suffering is not one of pity, but it is a lifting of the world's load of sin and trouble. The unity of one with another, the bearing of one another's burdens is brought about by our suffering with Christ.

It is true that Christ suffered directly in the stead of many and of us. He died outside the gates that He might sanctify the people with His own blood. Sin pierced His heart, and by the shedding of that blood, He made an atonement for our sins. Atonement in the Bible is always by blood, which represents the life of man poured out in satisfaction for guilt, and it is atonement alone that reconciles the sinner to God. True, those sufferings were substitutionary. He was the lonely Sufferer, the One suffering for the many. It was a sufficient atonement. It was one suffering for all, universal in kind. It was efficacious. He will save those for whom He died. It is the appeal of this suffering of Jesus unto us which says, "Let us therefore go forth unto Him without the camp, bearing His reproach." This sympathy for the lonely sufferer involves our bearing His reproach, knowing that He did His great work for us. We do not share in His atoning suffering but we suffer with Him in this world that we might be glorified with Him hereafter.

On the cross, we behold also a Christ who is sympathetically suffering for His own mother. There He succored her as well as substituted for her. If the Captain of our salvation was made perfect through suffering, suffering must be a part of life. We conceive of life as a trial. Man is born to trouble as the sparks fly upward. Suffering must add something to life and character, here and hereafter, and it is only the cross of Christ that gives the explanation of all this vicarious suffering in the world. Like as Christ succored His own mother from the cross, so all who will turn to Him can be succored in the time of their suffering and their need. With this perfect knowledge and sympathy for what we pass through, He can provide for our need. Thus His invitation is given to us to come boldly to the throne of grace and to ask for mercy and grace to help in time of need. It is true that Jesus empowers us to endure a pierced heart. No suffering for the believer can be too much, for all suffering is transformed into glory. Thus we endure these light afflictions, which are for the moment, because they work out a far more exceeding and eternal weight of glory. Mary's experience of a pierced heart tells us that she was compelled to suffer along with her Son and with others who are in need but that she was able to endure that affliction of heart in triumph because of the grace given to her by Christ, her Son and Lord.

Here, then, we see the noblest woman of all, the woman whose life fulfilled all that God promised to the women of the Old Testament who were good and precious and noble and true. Her Son was her own Saviour and Lord, just as He may be yours and He may be mine.

16

Martha

The Woman Who Made a House a Home

Jesus loved Martha (John 11:5).

In a little suburban village not far from a great city stood a fine old stone house. The way to this house from the city lay across a valley, up a rather steep incline, through gardens and groves of trees spotted with houses, until it crossed the top and began its descent on the other side. Shortly over the brow of the hill, from which one could get a commanding view of the entire countryside and the sea in the distance, was this pleasant little village, with its walled gardens, its lovely trees, its rare flowers, and its beautiful homes. Here merchants and professional people from the city had their residences. Most of these homes were large and spacious, built to remain in the family for years. The particular house in which we are interested had arched ceilings, large doors and hallways, a roof garden, outside porticos, and a private enclosure surrounded by a high wall. This house was forever to be associated with glorious memories.

A house may well be the center of interest not only for the family but also for a nation. When one stands in the Manning Manse, he feels the presence of many generations that have gone before in the long history of that old building. These pioneer colonists, whose descendants were Revolutionists, whose descendants fought in the Civil War, and whose descendants were perhaps at least interested in the outcome of the World Wars, with all of the cultural eras that passed between and were reflected in the individual characters of the heads of that household, seem very near to one as he handles the antiques and the relics of other days. It is no wonder that more than two hundred descendants will band themselves together in perpetuity to warrant the upkeep of that house.

Similarly, when one stands in the little home now encased in a national shrine at Hodgenville, Kentucky, he is directly conscious of the presence of Abraham Lincoln, whose early days were spent by the log fire in that home learning his sums of arithmetic and reading his books.

Again, as one stands in the great mansion on the Potomac called "Mount Vernon," he goes back farther still into a period when George and Martha Washington made their great sacrifices for the founding of a nation.

Or as one stands upon the beautiful porch of the columned Monticello at Charlottesville, Virginia, and looks down over the hill to the little law office in which Thomas Jefferson sat and from which he was called to his great office in the service of the country, one feels very close again to the life of a man who laid down ideas that have been considered cardinal American principles ever since.

Every home has its own story to tell. As one passes through the backwoods of New England and sees the old derelicts that once were inhabited by happy families and saw their joys and their tragedies, he feels strangely drawn and akin to another generation. Thus it is when one stands before the ruins of the old home in the village of Bethany.

There came a day when sorrow stalked through this particular house, when friends and relatives gathered to comfort the widow of the head of the household, when days of mourning were finished, and when the dear woman walked about those gardens and through those halls and chambers with a sense of loneliness that nothing could drive away. It was during these dark and dreary hours that the widow heard of a religious Teacher who gave beautiful sayings to His followers and who they claimed was able to comfort their hearts with a comfort that they could never know in any other way. One day she left her home and went to Jerusalem and stood at the edge of the multitude and listened to Him talk and heard Him say, "Come unto Me, all ye that labor and are heavy laden, and I will give you rest" (Matt. 11:28). She heard Him tell that He had come to bind up the broken-hearted, that His Father in heaven was interested in the least one who suffered, even in a sparrow who fell to the ground, and that nothing could occur to them, not even the falling of a hair from their heads, without His knowledge. Something within her heart responded, and she determined that this Man should be her Rabbi, her Teacher. As the days went on, she not only believed in Him and accepted His teachings concerning Himself as the Messiah, the sent One of Israel, but she also led her younger sister and her brother, all that she had left of her dear ones in the world, to a faith in Him such as hers.

Up until this profession of her faith and this committal of her life unto the Teacher she had not known what to do with her great home on the hill, but now she caught a vision of what that home could do. She would dedicate it to this Messiah and to His disciples as a place of refreshment and rest, as a retreat for teaching, as a gathering place for those who would listen and who would follow Him more closely. What wonderful stories might be told of the houses owned by widows, which have been dedicated to Christ, to the church, and to the work of the kingdom of God, of the groups who have gathered there to learn, to study the Bible, to hear the Word from some spiritual leader! How many have entered the hospitality of such homes to be changed in their inner characters and to go forth with faith into the world! All too little do we make use of our homes as places for the growth of the church and the influence of the Lord Jesus Christ, yet how sanctified are those few houses dedicated to these ends! What about that house of yours, that white elephant, that great derelict? Have you ever dedicated it to God and to God's work? Have you turned it over to the use of those who are the people of God for service? That house may become one of the centers of God's influence in your community.

That is exactly what this home at Bethany became. So we invite you to look at the *Home Over Which Martha Presided,* then at the *Home of Martha in Sorrow,* then, at the *Home of Martha in Joy.* We mention all this that you may remember Jesus in just such a setting on the day in which we think of Him as King.

I. The Home Over Which Martha Presided

There were many houses in and around Jerusalem, but only one of them was home for Jesus. When Jesus thought of Capernaum, home was the house of Peter's mother-in-law who had made Him welcome when He had been driven from Nazareth. When He thought of home at Cana of Galilee, it was the home of Nathanael. Whenever He thought of home near Jerusalem, it was the house of Martha in Bethany. In Martha's eyes, nothing in this house was good enough for the Master. Whenever the announcement was made, "The Master cometh," Martha felt that all hands must go to work to make the necessary arrangements.

And the Master came whenever He was tired and weary and in need of sympathy — the touch of a woman's hand. Men who are in public life, in conflict, in strife, under criticism, bearing burdens of others, love the place called home. It is their castle, their fortress, their resting-place, and happy are they when a good woman makes it a true home. Whenever the scribes and Pharisees and doctors of the law made life difficult for Jesus in Jerusalem, by questioning Him and ridiculing Him and pouring their contempt upon Him; when His tender humanity ached with sorrow and suffering; and when He was exceedingly burdened with the sins of those with whom He discoursed and for whom He labored, He walked out at eventide to Bethany, over the crown of the Mount of Olives.

There in Martha's house He found a haven of rest. This privilege of going to a place that shuts out the din and the harshness of the world, where love abides and where one is surrounded with those who are sympathetically and affectionately inclined, is one of the precious experiences of life. It is no wonder that Jesus loved the home of Martha of Bethany and that He habitually frequented it whenever He was in the vicinity of Jerusalem. Especially is this true when we realize that it is written of the Son of God that He had no place to lay His head. He was rejected in His own city. He was utterly dependent upon the kindness and the hospitality of friends. He often slept out-of-doors in the wilderness, wrapped only in His outer cloak, and when He approached Jerusalem, it was with joy that He thought of the home of Martha.

This hospitality of Martha for Christ is the New Testament counterpart of the Shunammite's hospitality for the prophet Elisha in the Old Testament (II Kings 4:8-37). If you recall, the prophet was in the habit of passing her door in his travels from Mount Carmel to Jezreel. So she inquired of her husband if it were not possible for them to prepare a chamber in the wall that might be called The Prophet's Chamber and where he might turn in at his own leisure and rest as he willed in passing. There he put simple furniture, such as a chair, a bed, and a table, and there the prophet stopped from time to time in his journey. Then there came the time of her need, when the son who had been born to her in fulfillment of the prophet's word fell on a day and died. The reward came to the Shunammite woman for her interest in and hospitality to the prophet. She made known her dire need unto him and through the prophet's intercession with God, the child was restored to her, well. In detail there is a great parallelism between this Old Testament story and the story of Martha, for Martha's brother Lazarus, probably also a younger person, fell sick and Martha sent for Christ, just as the Shunammite woman had sent for Elisha. When Christ came, though too late for any earthly help, He raised Lazarus from the dead. This was the fruit of her hospitality.

The first mention we have of Martha is in connection with a dinner party she prepared for Jesus and probably for some of His disciples (Luke 10: 38-42). The Lord was on His way from Capernaum to Jerusalem, and He passed by Bethany and turned in to the house of Martha, who received Him gladly. We are not told whether the disciples were entertained or not, but we suppose that they were. Thus it was that a great burden devolved upon Martha and upon her servants in order to prepare the evening meal. While Jesus was resting, she went about overseeing the directions in the home. The rooms were being straightened, the dinner was being prepared, the servants were hustling hither and yon, and Martha was bearing the full responsibility of all that she called the service. It was no easy task in a day of no delicatessens to prepare suddenly for unexpected guests. The words that describe Martha's condition are, "Cumbered about much serving." She had been bustling about from the time that Jesus arrived until nearly the time of the dinner. She was more tired than she knew, and her judgment was hardly clear. Her judgment was that of a woman overwrought, highly strung, and in a nervous state, typical of one who had worked too hard and now tried all the harder because of her own condition. Surely there is nothing to condemn in this. There is nothing reproachful. In fact, the woman was quite commendable, and whatever weakness or irritability rested in her was due to her physical condition rather than to her spiritual state. It was at this moment that the incident occurred which had left Martha's reputation somewhat in doubt in the church.

Throughout the day she had noticed that Mary, her younger sister, had done nothing but wait upon Christ and sit attentively at His feet as He taught. She had asked Him many questions that seemed to Martha to be of a speculative nature and altogether unnecessary when so much was to be done. Yet she had condoned her and allowed her to continue in her interests until almost the hour for the dinner. Then, as she passed by Mary and Jesus once more, for some unknown reason she felt provoked at her and interrupted their quiet talk with a rude question, saying, "Master, carest Thou not that my sister hath left me to serve alone? Bid her, therefore, that she help me." How many times this particular incident could be repeated in almost every home! Yet Jesus, knowing perfectly the spiritual condition and the life of both women, quietly responded, "Martha, Martha, thou art careful and troubled about many things; but one thing is needful, and Mary hath chosen that good part which shall not be taken away from her." We remember that when the apostles in the early church became cumbered about much serving of the tables, it occurred to them that it was not meet that they should leave the Word of God and do this work. Therefore, they appointed deacons who were ordained to accomplish this task (Acts 6). Wherever a minister of the Word of God leaves his primary task to take up the secondary task of serving, even though they be matters of charity and of common kindness, he nevertheless is not doing a commendable thing. He has not chosen the best part.

Martha's work was just as necessary as the work Mary performed, and Jesus did not tell her not to do that work. He did not rebuke her for doing it. He merely emphasized that one work was better than another. Every housewife or housemaid who does her work as unto the Lord is serving the Lord Jesus Christ. Every man in his carpenter shop or in his business may be serving the Lord Jesus Christ there just as well as someone else whom the Lord has delegated to a different field is serving Him there. Dr. Abraham Kuiper says that in the church of Christ some busy themselves with silver, others with gold, and still others with mere wood and stone, using Paul's expression. We can say that the difference between Mary and Martha is that the former worked in gold and the latter in silver, but certainly all are not to work in gold, for he who works in silver is doing his duty. Supposing John the Evangelist to be one who worked in pure gold and Mark to be one who worked in silver, Mark would have been shirking his responsibility had he attempted to imitate John in the teaching he recorded. Thus it is here also. God placed two sisters in Lazarus' family. He gave them appropriate talents and accordingly had given to each a peculiar calling. For that reason, each acquitted herself of her responsibility only when she followed her own particular path. In His reprimand of Martha, Jesus did not tell her to do as Mary did, but when Martha valued her own silver more highly than Mary's gold, when she told Jesus, "Tell Mary to assist me in serving," then Jesus felt that she had to be enlightened. It was then that He told her that Mary had not chosen to do the less desirable but the more desirable thing. Martha had no right to look with disdain upon Mary's quiet, peaceful, faith-engendered spiritual life. And those who follow the pathway of Mary have no right to look down upon Martha with disdain. Both occupations are desirable. It is highly blessed that we have some who are engaged in deeds of mercy, but it is also necessary that some be engaged in the work of the kingdom of God, which is the direct preaching of the Gospel of Jesus Christ, and each in his place is best. Martha in her own place was certainly supreme.

II. The Home of Martha in Sorrow

Suffering plays a large part in making a house a home. When a family moves into a new home, it is highly improbable that they will ever feel quite as much at home in the new house until it has had some session of illness, some crisis, or some experience of need. Then it is that the walls seem to enter into one's own experience to sympathize and to partake of his life. Perhaps some of us are more sentimental about a house than others, but as Edgar Guest says, "It takes a heap o' living to make a house a home." When you have planted the shrubbery that grows around your house and tended the garden and raised the blades of grass; when you have built the stone wall that encases your garden; when you have enclosed your porch; when you have entertained in your living-room; when you have cleaned it and remodeled it year after year; and when you have sat through the long quiet hours of the night waiting by the side of the bed of some loved one, whether mother or daughter, until the morning light should break upon a face that would respond for the better or for the worse then that house has become a home. When the suffering and the living and the loving seem to saturate its very walls and fill it with a heap of memories, it becomes a place that wherever you are in the world you will always look back to and call home. Perhaps Mother is no longer there. Perhaps sister has long since been married and brother gone away, but still it is home. Can you forget the mental picture drawn by Margaret Mitchell of Scarlet O'Hara returning to her home, Tara, after Sherman's invasion of Georgia and the burning of the great mansions along the way? She found the stock gone, the furniture stolen, the barns burned, and nothing but the bare building yet standing. Still as she stood upon the barren ground and looked across the hills at the noble building, she cried, "Tara," for it was home. Either cottage or a mansion, however humble, "there is no place like home."

Now came the time of suffering and sorrow for the household at Bethany during which Martha's protective strength was revealed. The story in the eleventh chapter of John is one of the touching and beautiful ones in the Scripture. Here we even learn that Jesus wept, and here Martha stands out with the majesty of a woman who knew how to conduct herself in the time of trouble and trial. The day came when Lazarus did not rise from his bed in the morning, when he called for his sisters and told them that he did not feel well. They tended him as many others have tended loved ones, thinking that their loved one was slightly ill and would soon be better, but as the days passed they soon saw that it was not as minor an ailment as they had supposed. Lazarus was rapidly slipping down-hill. Then it was, in the fear which was almost a premonition, that they thought of the Lord Jesus and decided to send to Him. The message was terse and short, only, "Lord, behold he whom Thou lovest is sick," but it was sufficient to tell the story. These women knew that if Jesus could come, all would be well with their brother.

For a reason into which we do not need to enter for the purpose of this discussion, Jesus tarried for several days after the message came to Him in the section called Perea. Then, when He knew that Lazarus was dead, He turned His face toward Bethany. Meanwhile, we may well imagine how that Mary and Martha alternately took turns watching the bedside of Lazarus and going to their portico to look down the long road toward Jericho to see if Jesus were coming or if any company that might be the company of Jesus were on its way. Then the time came when Martha, weeping, made her way out to her sister Mary, standing looking toward the east, and broke the news that Lazarus was dead.

Four days passed, during which they and their friends had Lazarus embalmed and buried in the cave not far from their home on the hill. Then, with much misgiving, they continued to wait for the coming of Jesus. During this time Martha recovered more quickly than Mary, for as soon as she heard that Jesus was coming, she went and met Him, but Mary sat still in the house, buried in her grief and in her mourning. When Martha came to Jesus, she said, "Lord, if Thou hadst been here my brother had not died, but I know that even now whatsoever Thou wilt ask of God, God will give it Thee." What a remarkable faith that is! What a triumphant statement! What a confession to the Lord! Her faith was so great that Jesus merely said, "Thy brother shall rise again." Then Martha replied (and note the "I know"), "I know that he shall rise again in the resurrection at the last day." Here was a woman with a certainty of faith that declared that she had not seen the last of her brother and that they would be united once again. But Jesus said, "I am the resurrection and the life. He that believeth in Me, though he were dead, yet shall he live; and whosoever liveth and believeth in Me shall never die. Believest thou this?" Still in faith, Martha said, "Yes, Lord, I believe that Thou art the Christ, the Son of God which should come into the world." Here we catch a vision of a woman who had as great a faith and who made as great a statement of that faith as any disciple made before the resurrection of Christ. She believed, and she was ready to act upon that belief.

We have no record that Jesus spoke and asked for Mary, but we read that Martha went to Mary and said to her, "The Master is come and calleth for thee." This we take to be some of the protective kindness Martha manifested toward her sister Mary during these days, for the news of the arrival of the Lord Jesus and that He wanted her caused Mary to go into His presence immediately. There she, too, said what Martha had said, "Lord, if Thou hadst been here my brother had not died," and with that she left her confession and broke into weeping. Surely it was this suffering of Mary as much as anything else that caused the tears to come from the eyes of our blessed Lord, even though He knew that He was to raise Lazarus from the dead. Thus it was that these women received the answer to their faith. At the command of the Lord, the stone was rolled away from the grave and, though Martha protested that already decay had set in, Jesus spoke, "Lazarus, come forth." Then the greatest miracle of all that were performed by Christ occurred—the body of the man Lazarus came forth, bound hand and foot with grave clothes, and his face covered about with a napkin, and Jesus commanded those standing around about to loose him and let him go. Lazarus, a dead man, was raised to life again. The scene of reunion and joy can only be imagined and not described.

III. The Home of Martha in Joy

The last picture we get of Martha and of her home is on the day preceding the triumphal entry of Christ into Jerusalem as King (Matt. 26:6-13; John 12:1-11). It was on the Sabbath evening before the Passover, when Christ was again entertained at Bethany with a dinner party in the home of Simon the leper, at which Martha had control of the serving. The central personage of interest at this dinner was Lazarus who, the record tells us twice, was the one who had been dead, whom Christ had raised from the dead. Lazarus was the standing miracle who was convincing the Jews constantly that Jesus was the Christ, their Messiah. This time, not only Jesus was present but all of His disciples. Together with Lazarus they sat at this large table partaking of the feast. We have no means of knowing what the conversation was at this particular dinner, but we may be sure that it included such topics as "the spiritual meaning of the Passover" which was soon to be celebrated, whereby the Lord God had provided for the people of God a means of atonement for the forgiveness of their sins. It probably included that great subject of prayer about which the disciples had asked the Lord the last time they had visited at Bethany, when they said, "Lord, teach us to pray." It may even have included some suggestions by Christ of the approaching end of His own life, their concern about it, and their failure to understand the cause of His death. Did Lazarus tell them about his experience during death, or did he find that all such former experiences were forgotten when he returned into this world? We have no means of knowing, but we know that he must have conversed with them because of the prominence given to him as one who sat at the table. In him the disciples had evidence enough to seal their faith in Christ regardless of whatever occurred in the future, knowing that He was God's messenger, God's Son.

In this memorable season of the Passover, Martha gave her expression of gratitude for and celebration of the raising of her brother Lazarus and the restoring of him to her home in the presentation of this great feast. Once again we find her building with her works of silver rather than works of gold. To how much of the conversation Martha listened we do not know, but we know that she served. This time it does not tell that she was cumbered about much serving. Martha now performed the work to which God had called her without the unnecessary nervous excitability. Let all the Marthas in the church take comfort in the fact that the Lord acknowledges their service and that He accepts their service. The matter most important to Him is how the service is performed, whether in peace and in faith or in turmoil and unbelief.

Mary's expression of gratitude was different from Martha's. Mary had probably thought a long time what she could do. Her sister was giving the great dinner. Lazarus could sit at the table and express himself to the Lord Jesus, but Mary had no talent at all except that of listening, so Mary took the costly ointment that had been purchased, perhaps at the price of her savings, and brought the alabaster container into the great room during the feast. There she cracked the box and poured the ointment over His head so that the aroma filled the house with pleasant odors. Hers was to be a service of adoration and worship. In fact, one surmises that Mary had a premonition of the coming death of Christ, or at least that she acted in faith upon His own teaching that He was soon to die. That Mary was rebuked by Judas and the disciples is beside the point here, for they did not understand. But Jesus did, and He said, "Let her alone: against the day of My burying hath she kept this. Wherever this gospel shall be preached throughout the whole world this also that she hath done shall be spoken of for a memorial of her." Truly, wherever the Gospel has been preached we have remembered Mary for her act of adoration and love, but we have also remembered Martha for her act of courtesy and hospitality and love to her Lord. One was as great as the other within the sphere of each life.

Happy is it that we may remember Jesus on the first day of the last week in such a setting as this, among His friends, among loved ones, among disciples. We see Him present in and blessing the house of those whom He loved. Thereafter, Martha, Mary, and Lazarus could always say, "Christ is the Head of this house, the unseen Guest at every meal, the silent listener to every conversation," for Christ was really there.

Have you invited Jesus Christ into your home? Is the house in which you live the home of the Lord? Because He dwells in you, does He dwell there? Do you begin the day with

Him, either in family worship or at least grace at the table? Have you honored Him in all things, and do you obey Him and follow His guidance during the day? Do you minister unto Him, and do you sit at His feet to worship Him? If you accept Jesus into your home, you will find that sometimes He will rebuke you for your choice of the lesser instead of the better thing, but He will love you in the midst of it all. In His gentleness He will make your house a heavenly home on earth until you may go to the Father's house in which there are many mansions, one prepared for you.

17

Mary Magdalene

THE WOMAN WHO COULD NOT FORGET

> *The first day of the week cometh Mary Magdalene early,*
> *when it was yet dark, to the sepulcher* (John 20:).

Of all the women in the Bible, the highest place, next to
Mary the mother of Jesus, must be accorded to Mary Magdalene. She took the most prominent part and is given the most
prominent place in the Passion narratives of our Lord. She takes
this high place because she could never forget what Jesus Christ
had done for her.

Women who cannot forget are often trouble-makers. They
cannot overlook nor forget slights or wrongs that have been
done to them, or even opposition to their will. Their desire
for vengeance causes incalculable suffering in the world. Remember Jezebel's determination to be avenged of Elijah, and
the anger of Herodias at Baptist John, ending in his death!

Other women, however, can never forget the good that is
done to them; they always want to repay that good and become a blessing to the world. Such a woman was the wife of
Chuza, Herod's steward, whose name was Joanna. She had
been cured by our Lord, either of possession by an evil spirit
or of a disease, and out of her gratitude she attached herself
to that body of women who accompanied Him upon His journeys and ministered to Him of their substance and who were
faithful at the cross and even on the resurrection morning, for
she came with Mary Magdalene to the tomb to anoint the
body with spices. Another is Martha, whose life we have al

ready studied and who because of the Lord's goodness to her family, including the raising of Lazarus from the dead, could never do enough for Him by way of service. But greater than either of these is the one who is the subject of this chapter, namely, Mary Magdalene.

Of all the grateful women in the Bible who could not forget, Mary Magdalene is the outstanding person. Therefore, she may stand for us as the symbol of the worship of the Christ by women who cannot forget what Christ has done for them. Hers is the single case that presents the resurrection in all of its historic and its spiritual phases to us. In her own life we see the spiritual resurrection from a life condemned to bondage and through her eyes we can see the physical resurrection of Christ. Centering our attention upon Mary and the part she played in the resurrection, may I suggest for your consideration, first, *What Mary Could Not Forget;* second, *The Person Whom Mary Could Not Forget;* and third, *What Mary Would Have Missed Had She Forgotten.*

1. WHAT MARY COULD NOT FORGET

We are introduced to Mary Magdalene in the verses immediately following the story of Jesus and the woman who was a sinner (Luke 8:1-3; 7:37ff). This has resulted in Mary often being identified with the woman who was a sinner, but the Scripture only says that Mary had been healed of evil spirits and infirmities, seven devils going out from her. There are three theories concerning Mary's past.

The first theory identifies Mary with the sinful woman. In the great Zwinger Gallery in Dresden, there is a picture by Coreggio of the Magdalene. She lies in a cave, still marked by the badges of her sin but now reading from the Scripture. Her long tresses fall about her full neck and exposed bosom, with every indication given of voluptuous practices from which she has just now been snatched. Before her appearance has changed, with the exception of the look in her eyes, she has her attention riveted upon the Scripture. The idea portrayed is that Mary was the woman who was a sinner and had only now returned to a lonely place to be confirmed in the change wrought by Jesus at the feast of Simon. This conception of Mary is quite general in the Christian world, so that the word "Magdalene" has come to represent a fallen woman; we have houses of Magdalene, homes for such poor souls who are victims of social evil. The Roman Church has done more than any other influence to fasten this stigma upon Mary by the means of the practice of a very worthy charity. Beginning in the fourteenth century, they established a series of monasteries called "Magdelene Houses," in each of which were three congregations, those of St. Magdalene, those of St. Martha, and those of St. Lazarus, which reveals the Roman identification of Mary Magdalene, the fallen woman, and Mary of Bethany as one person. There may be some question about the identification of the fallen woman and Mary of Bethany, but certainly this fallen woman cannot be Mary Magdalene. Since that date, Magdalene houses have been established all over the world.

Though Roman Catholicism identifies Mary Magdalene and the woman who was a sinner, most Protestant scholars give good grounds for not identifying them. Certainly a woman who was demon possessed is not one who would be profitable in that oldest trade of the world. That fallen woman was saved at a house of Simon, the Pharisee, who had invited Jesus and His disciples to a feast, but had omitted all of the common courtesies and amenities of the social order, such as the kiss of salvation, the water for the washing of the feet, and the oil for the anointing of the head. During the feast, this woman of the streets entered and made her way directly to the couch of Jesus. Simon did not stop her, thinking probably Christ would, but Christ paid her no attention. She must have been touched somewhere by some of His teaching and have had her heart changed, and now she came to express her gratitude to Him. Kneeling by His couch, she washed His feet with her tears and wiped them with the hairs of her head and then anointed them with precious oil, which undoubtedly was purchased of the reward of her iniquity and consumed much of her substance. Jesus then used the incident as a parable to teach the unforgiving and supercilious Simon a lesson. He said: "There was a certain creditor which had two debtors; the one owed five hundred pence and the other fifty, and when they had nothing to pay, he frankly forgave them both. Tell me, therefore, which of them will love him most?" Simon replied, "I suppose that he to whom he forgave most." Jesus then said, "Thou has rightly judged" and, turning to the woman, He continued, "Seest thou this woman? I entered thine house and thou gavest Me no water for My feet, but she hath washed My feet with tears and wiped them with the hairs of her head. Thou gavest Me no kiss; but this woman since the time I came in hath not ceased to kiss My feet. My head with oil thou didst not anoint: but this woman hath anointed My feet with ointment. Wherefore I say unto thee, her sins, which are many, are forgiven; for she loved much: but to whom little is forgiven, the same loveth little." Then to the woman He said, "Thy faith hath saved thee; go in peace." Whether this woman was Mary or not, only heaven can reveal, but she believed on the Lord Jesus Christ and that belief was the source of love that was poured out upon Him, in due humility. Perhaps we are wrong and this woman was Mary Magdalene. If so, all honor to her as she abandoned her illicit and shameful trade and became a true follower of the Lord Jesus Christ.

The second interpretation, and that to which we adhere, is that Mary was a lunatic and demon possessed. Rather than a fallen woman, we think of her as an afflicted woman, suffering from an unfortunate condition prevalent in Jesus' day. We recall the story of the demoniac of Gadara, which was just across the lake from Magdala, where tradition says there were many demon possessed and where Christ healed at least one who had lived naked and who had broken his chains and dwelt among the caves, and frightened all comers (Mark 5: 1-20). This gives us a picture of what Mary must have been like. Think of this woman of delicate frame, now irrational and with lunatic outlook, with wild eyes and disheveled hair, either living in the tombs or haunting the outskirts of the village until Jesus found her. If you would see people like that today, go to the insane asylums, listen to their wails, see their sense- less, vacant eyes, listen to their talk, watch them leap, dance, or crawl, and you will have an idea of what Mary was like. Whether demon possession was the same as insanity or a particular manifestation of the evil world at the same time that heaven put forth its best and sent Jesus into the world, we cannot be sure, but out of Mary went seven demons. Perhaps men had driven her, as many weaker vessels in our day have been driven to insanity, by cruelty. A domineering father, a thoughtless husband, exposure to extreme calamity, or some other cause may have lain back of it, but the people of Mag- dala called her "Mary" in scorn, as the town crazy woman, but when Jesus first saw her and realized what this woman in her rational condition would become, He said, "Mary," in a different way which she could never forget. Into her dim, distant look there came focused reason and understanding, followed by a balanced appreciation and love. Mary was healed and was returned, clothed and in her right mind, to her home and family. No wonder that Mary's gratitude to the Lord Jesus was great!

There is yet a third interpretation of the history of Mary, which is advanced by Dr. MacLaren. He believed that these seven demons were figurative representations of the seven sins of Dante, which are to be found in the hearts of us all, and that Mary was neither a great sinner nor was she a maniac, but that she was perfectly delivered in this world from the evil that hounds each of us, namely, pride, envy, anger, lascivious- ness, covetousness, intemperance, and spiritual sloth. That old Scottish preacher testified that he could never find those demons completely vanished from his heart and life and that anyone so delivered must have been a great saint. Mary be- came just such a saint. If this interpretation is true, it is the correct interpretation of the power of Christ to quicken us from our trespasses and sins to a new life. This kind of resur- rection, we all need to know. What Jesus did for Mary, He has done for multitudes throughout history.

It is quite clear that whatever the original condition of Mary, she was thoroughly and completely changed by the power of Christ. If she was a lunatic, then the first time that Jesus said, "Mary," her reason returned to her and she looked out upon the world with rational and sensible eyes and countenance. If she was a sinner of the streets, then when Jesus told her, "Go in peace; thy faith hath saved thee," a transformation occurred that was a mighty miracle. If through listening to His teaching she was delivered from the mortal sins that plague the lives of most people, she stands as a monument of the grace of God. Whatever Mary's past, her change is an illustration of a spiritual resurrection in the life of an individual. Paul said, "You hath He quickened, who were dead in trespasses and sins" (Eph. 2:1), and then he calls this resurrection. Undoubtedly it is a resurrection, but it is not the only resurrection. There later arose some in the church who claimed that this was the only resurrection and that the resurrection spoken of in the Bible was just for those who are Christians, but Paul declared it to be an error. However, we may know this great spiritual resurrection. This is the demonstration that Christ is living today. Whenever a character is changed, whenever a sinner is transformed from the kingdom of darkness to the kingdom of light, when habits are broken and a new life begins, we have evidence of the fact that Christ has risen from the dead and is living.

Immediately after Mary was changed, she entered upon a ministry of gratitude to Christ. She joined the little group of women who, as Matthew says, "ministered unto Him of their substance." Very probably Mary came from a family of much substance and now she not only dedicated her person but she dedicated her possessions to Him and to His servants. Christ and His disciples had to live in some way, and these women probably provided the means for their sustenance. It would be well to follow Mary's example, for we can certainly do no better when Christ has bestowed upon us spiritual and moral healing than to give both ourselves and our possessions to Him as gifts upon His altar. Mary did not cease her ministry with the giving of her substance. She also devoted her service to Christ. Mary was faithful to Him when all others failed. The narrative implies that she was the inspiring spirit among all of the faithful women, for she is always named first in the group, whether at the cross or at the tomb, by all of the evangelists. When others had fled from Christ at the time of His capture and then of His trial, proving that they could not stand with Him, Mary proved that she could (Matt. 27:56). When the morning light dawned on that Day of the Passover and the multitudes assembled at the Gabbatha, word came to Mary that the Master was arrested and was being accused before Pilate. Thither she went with all haste to witness, to help, and to encourage Jesus, but helpless, she stood back on the edge of the scene, prevented by the soldiers from coming nearer. It was there that she saw all of the events that led to Golgotha, but there was no fear on Mary's part. Even at the cross, when others mocked Him and ridiculed Him and probably were very hostile to any followers who might be there, yet Mary stayed. When Jesus sent His own mother, Mary the Virgin, away with John the Beloved, still Mary Magdalene remained. Rubens, in one of his great paintings, depicts Mary as helping Joseph of Arimathea and Nicodemus to remove Christ's body from the cross and participating in the labors of love as it was bound and prepared for burial. Then she followed the little procession to the tomb and observed all that was done, weeping. She and Mary, the mother of Joseph, particularly marked where the body was laid and how the tomb was closed before they left because of the coming of the Sabbath, which they must spend in their homes (Mark 15:47).

Never was a sadder Sabbath spent in the history of the world than that when the Son of God lay in the tomb. During this Sabbath, Mary was occupied not only with sorrow and remembering but also with the preparation of a love gift that she might again minister to her Lord on the first day of the week. Then she and the women returned to the tomb to perform a deed of gratitude and affection as the last symbol of her loyalty. Mary impresses one as desiring that her life should adequately express her gratitude. This may have been unconscious and natural to her, but it nevertheless was present. Surely every Christian should examine his own life according to his profession of benefit and blessing from the Lord to see if he has forgotten those things in the action he manifests before the world.

II. THE PERSON WHOM SHE COULD NOT FORGET

One of the strange things about bereavement is that when we have lost a loved one, the particular characteristics of that person stand out more clearly than they did when he was living. We can remember one particular thing he was in the habit of doing or one particular expression that endeared him to us. Such thoughts must have occupied Mary's meditation on the Sabbath. She probably thought of the person of the human Jesus, of His sufferings on the cross, and of the transformation He had wrought in her life and that was the first impression she had of Him.

There is no doubt that Mary was interested in the human Jesus. The prophet Isaiah said, "There is no beauty that we should desire Him" (Isa. 53:2). Others could not see the beauty that was in Jesus, but Mary saw that beauty, and she loved it and Him. To Mary, Jesus was truly the Lily of the Valley, the Rose of Sharon, the Bright and Morning Star. He was the sunrise and the sunset of her soul. The dignity, the authority, the mercy, the kindness, and the endless service Christ performed in utter devotion to the will of God had utterly captivated Mary. She was enthralled with Him. For Mary, life without Jesus was meaningless. It was not worth living. It was empty and void. It was worse than useless. Mary loved in Christ that which others hated, namely, His perfect goodness and righteousness. It is in this way that Christ reveals the character of persons. If His perfection and His righteousness call forth your love and your affection, happy are you, but if it calls forth your hatred and your repugnance, woe unto you, for then you are full of sin. Sinful men do not love Christ, for His perfections show up their imperfections.

It is perfectly possible that the fleshly Christ may have been too much in Mary's mind, but how could she separate the two? She was devoted to His body from beginning to end, so that when she once saw the resurrected Christ, she fell at His feet, wishing to clasp them to her again, now to keep Him forever, for Mary was unable to distinguish between the spiritual and the physical Christ.

Thus we may understand the sorrow of Mary in her sense of loss at the death of Jesus. Her woman's mind did not think of what it meant to the cause, that Jesus had died. She had no interest in the kingdom, as the disciples did, or in power, or in politics, or the breaking of the Roman yoke. She was interested only in fellowship, and love, and communion. His death interrupted her fellowship, and she was overwhelmed with the sense that she would see Him no more, and this was too much for her. Mary simply could not get her mind away from the tomb in which the body of Christ reposed. She loved Jesus, and Jesus was dead. Thus Mary's love lingered on the body of Christ. Perhaps you cannot understand that now, but some day you will, in the hour of bereavement. Few are the emancipated souls that can love the spirit of the person disassociated from the body. Mary had not reached that high position yet.

On that Sabbath Day, the remembrance of the sufferings of Christ on the cross must have weighed on Mary. She had seen everything, from the trial at the Gabbatha to the tomb. She saw all those events — His mock trial, His refusal to defend Himself, Pilate publicly washing his hands to clear himself of the guilt, the result of the scourging as they thrust Him forth bleeding and crowned with thorns, saying, "Behold the Man." Surely if ever Mary wept, it was then. Mary followed as near as possible outside the ring of soldiers as they led Him along the Via Dolorosa to crucify Him. She was one of those weeping women to whom Jesus turned and said as He went along, "Daughters of Jerusalem, weep not for Me, but weep for yourselves . . . for if they do these things in a green tree, what shall be done in a dry?" (Luke 23:28-31.) Mary had seen Him fall under the cross, receive the lashes from the soldiers, but, unable to go on, transfer His burden to Simon the Cyrenian. Then she had stood by the cross during the entire crucifixion and saw Him in agony. Mary could not forget the words He had spoken there, words praying for the forgiveness of His crucifiers and tormentors, words of promise to a dying thief, words of petition unto a Father who seemed not to hear. Yes, Mary was burdened by the sufferings of the person of Christ.

Moreover, she knew these to be unjust. She knew that He had never wronged a soul and that He was hated only because He freed men from the yoke of the law, from fear, from disease, as she had been freed. She was sure in her own mind that He never claimed to be a king of anything but of truth and of righteousness. He even refused to be made king when they wanted to force Him to become king. He was no rival of Caesar, not even of the high priest, and yet His friends and His followers and all those whom He had helped and healed and befriended had deserted Him. Why such events were permitted to happen troubled Mary severely, just as they have troubled many who have seen the just suffer ever since the cross. It is possible that the vicariousness of Calvary may have faintly dawned upon Mary's mind, but she had no certainty of it. Only the thought that Jesus was dying for sinful men as their substitute, bearing their sin and the penalty of their evil and the curse of the law, can explain the cross, and only the vicariousness of the suffering of the righteous is able to place meaning into it today. We are able, because of the cross of Christ, to endure that which we are called upon to endure when we innocently suffer.

No doubt much of that day was also spent in remembrance of what this Person had wrought in her life. She vividly sensed the peace, the joy, and the purpose that had been substituted for her aimless, distracted, tumultuous living of other days. How blessed it had been to walk with Him during these three years! Was it all to end now? Was she again to be enmeshed in her sin, in her failures, in her evil, in her distractions of mind, and in her sorrow? Now that He was dead, was she again to go back to the old life? No, a thousand times no!

She would now live as if He were with her always. Nevertheless, there was a very real fear with Mary that if Jesus were dead and remained dead, He could no longer deliver her from her present enemies, from evil within and without, and in that Mary was right. It is folly to think that anything but a resurrected, living Christ can give deliverance from sin today. If Jesus remained in the tomb, or if His body was stolen by anyone and did not rise from the dead, then Christ is not a deliverer; then He has not defeated our great enemy and we have real reason to fear. Mary sensed the fact that a dead Jesus would declare the cross to be a defeat and the end of the cause, both for her and for the Christian movement, and so it would.

III. What Mary Would Have Missed Had She Forgotten

Had Mary not been the grateful woman she was, she would have missed many things. First of all, she would have missed the revelation of the resurrected Christ. But Mary did not forget and was the first in faithfulness and hence, the first in reward; for unto Mary, Christ first appeared after His resurrection. Wonderful were those events of that first Easter morning, and in them all Mary played a prominent part. She came with Mary of Galilee and Joanna and other women following, bearing the spices that they might anoint the body of Jesus, and worrying over who should move the stone for them. When they came to the tomb, saw the soldiers overcome and lying upon the ground, an angel sitting upon the stone, and heard the words, "He is not here, but risen; go and tell His disciples," like a flash Mary turned and went to tell Peter and John, while Mary of Galilee went on to the women, who in turn came to investigate the tomb and then left in order to inform the rest of the disciples. Meanwhile Mary, Peter, and John returned to the tomb to see what had happened to the body of Jesus. Peter entered, and I suppose the others followed, where they saw the linen clothes lying and the napkin folded, and John believed Jesus had risen from the dead. After the disciples left, Mary was alone, weeping and wondering what had happened to the body of Jesus (John 20:11-18). She did not yet believe either the message of the angels or the evidence that her Lord was risen. Then it was that she saw someone approaching her whom she took to be the gardener, and not recognizing Him through her tears, she asked, "If thou hast taken Him away, tell me and I will take Him." Suddenly she heard a voice say, "Mary!" and she knew it was the voice of her Lord. She fell at His feet to grasp Him and hold Him forever, now that He had been restored to her. Surely this Mary was no more mistaken in her vision of the resurrected Christ than were the other disciples in His later appearances. She went to the disciples later in the day and affirmed that it was even so, that the resurrected Lord had appeared to her. Whatever you may think about the resurrection, these appearances of Christ cannot be reasoned away. They were seen by too many people, in too many places, and on too many different times in order to be treated lightly.

While Mary lay at Jesus' feet, an incident occurred that presents the Christian conception of Christ. He said to her, "Touch Me not, for I am not yet ascended, but go to My disciples and tell them I go before them into Galilee. I ascend unto My Father and to your Father." How shall we interpret this passage, which says, "Touch Me not," when a few moments later seemingly Christ allowed the other women to touch Him? Some say that Mary would have clung to the body to keep Jesus with her forever, to hold this fleshly knowledge and experience. Mary needed gentle instruction that Christ was about to assume a new relationship and that she should not seek to hold Him to this earth. Paul once said, "Though we have known Christ after the flesh, yea, now, henceforth know we Him no more" (II Cor. 5:16). It is possible to have a fleshly knowledge of Christ and to have a spiritual knowledge of Christ. When Paul held the fleshly knowledge, he persecuted Jesus. When he had the spiritual knowledge, he loved Him and served Him as a disciple. In the flesh, Christ could be with only one person at one place at one time, but the ascended Christ is omnipresent and with us always. Augustine suggested that now we should touch Him with the hands of faith and not with the hands of the flesh.

Another thing that Mary would have missed had she forgotten, was being commissioned as the first messenger of the resurrected Lord. She was the first to hear the heavenly tidings of the Gospel complete with the resurrection. This Gospel vindicated by the resurrection is the greatest message that ever was committed to man and was ever preached. Paul told Timothy to be unashamed of the Gospel of Christ because he could remember that God raised Him from the dead. With the resurrection there is no need ever to be ashamed of this great Gospel, for it is vindicated before the reason of men. Mary carried the news to the disciples.

Mary was the herald of the era of grace, of the church, of missions, of world evangelism, of an ascended and glorified Christ, who had entered upon the throne of His spiritual kingdom. She announced first what has called forth our highest devotion and service ever since.

We have considered Mary as the woman who could not forget. Let us also recall that the Lord's Supper was established by Christ as a symbol of remembrance. He said, "Do this in remembrance of me" (Luke 22:19). Just as He is at the center of the Lord's Supper, so He should be at the center of our Christian faith and of our own lives. Mary takes her high place among women and among Christians because she remembered Him at all times, in all places. Can you, then, my friend, forget what He did for you when He died upon the cross and rose from the dead? Can you forget what He is now as Savior, Priest, and King, at the right hand of God? Can you forget what His purposes are in this world in the redemption of man? If you have forgotten, cast yourself at His feet now, and with a touch of faith cling to Christ and worship Him in gratitude and love.

> *Lest I forget Gethsemane,*
> *Lest I forget Thine agony,*
> *Lest I forget Thy love to me,*
> *Lead me, O Lord, to Calvary.*

Yes, and lead me, Lord, to Thy feet in worship.

18

The Gentile Woman

THE WOMAN WHO PUT PRAYER INTO PRACTICE

O woman, great is thy faith: be it unto thee even as thou wilt. And her daughter was made whole from that very hour (Matt. 15:28).

We believers stand in constant need of instruction in prayer. He who prays knows that there is a mystery connected with it. This mystery is suggested in this story of divine silence to the petition of a needy woman and in the reward which her prayer received because it was accompanied by faith.

Most people who pray are conscious of their inability in this realm. The disciples were very conscious of this when they saw and heard Jesus praying. As a result, they said, "Lord, teach us to pray" (Luke 11:1). Paul experienced the same sense of futility and inability in prayer. He said, "For we know not what we should pray for as we ought" (Rom. 8:26). And we Christians who have the full light of divine revelation on this subject of prayer as given to us in the Bible still find a great mystery connected with it. We must admit that we have unanswered prayers, that we have prayers the answers to which have been deferred, and that on other occasions we have remarkable answers to prayer. Hence, we need more and more to be assisted in our prayers by the Holy Spirit.

The incentive to praying is given to us in the Bible commands, exhortations, promises and examples. The Lord Jesus said, "Men ought always to pray, and not to faint." He challenged men by saying, "Ask, and it shall be given you; seek, and ye shall find; knock, and it shall be opened unto you"

(Matt. 7:7). He promises that "what things soever ye desire, when ye pray, believe that ye receive them, and ye shall have them" (Mark 11:24). His parables often were devoted to illustrating the practice of prayer and He Himself gave the most prominent example of one who prayed.

Instruction in the practice of prayer is concentrated in Luke 11:1-13. There we learn from the lips of the Lord Jesus the practice of prayer, the pattern of prayer, persistence in prayer, progression in prayer, and promise of prayer. This is the most extensive treatment of prayer given in the Bible and it comes from the highest authority, namely, the Lord Jesus Himself. Similar to it is the passage in James 5:13-18. There James gives the principles of effective praying which we shall later expound. In all this instruction in prayer we find that faith takes its place in prayer as it does in religion. Without such faith it is impossible to come to God, or to please God, or to move God, but with faith we find that the heroes in the roster of faith abound in the practice of prayer. Abraham interceded for Sodom (Gen. 18:23-33), Moses interceded for the condemned Israelites (Exod. 32:30-35), Samuel interceded for Saul (I Sam. 16:1, 2). In like manner, Elijah interceded for Israel and brought about a revival which gave it another chance. In all these cases we see the place of faith in prayer.

The Practice of Prayer

The passage in James 5:13-18 dealing with the basic principles in practice may be divided into the exhortations to prayer, the experience in prayer and the efficacy in prayer. James opens the passage by referring to those who are afflicted with tribulation, temptation and trial and who are in perplexity as to the way out. He suggests, "Let him pray." This is the answer to the basic need of each of us in similar circumstances. He then raises the question as to whether any are merry, buoyed up with excitement, with stimulus and enjoyment. These he advises to sing psalms, that is, to pray the prayer of gratitude by a happy response to their environment. He then raises the question concerning those who are sick. Since sickness is sooner or later the lot of every man and woman, it is appropriate for us to examine what James says about this circumstance. He exhorts the believers to call for the elders of the church so that they may pray over the sick person, anointing him with oil in the name of the Lord. Some branches of the church practice anointing oil for the purpose of healing the sick today. It is my opinion that this should only be done when the individual sick person has faith enough to ask for the elders of the church to come and to pray with him in order that by the sign of anointing and by the intercession of the elders, healing might be mediated to the individual.

In my years of pastoral ministry I have anointed numerous people in response to their request of faith. Always this was done in the presence of the elders who joined in prayer for the healing of the individual. I think of one of our returned missionaries who was suffering dreadfully from cancer and for whom we prayed. Her cancer was not healed but she never had any further pain until the day of her death. We have had cases in which people have been healed in answer to prayer without anointing. We have had other cases when we have anointed and prayed and the person was not healed. Generally speaking, anointing with oil in the New Testament or the laying on of hands were ceremonies confined to the Jewish church. When the church broke beyond the bonds of the Jewish people, these were not universally practiced.

James promised those who practiced prayer that the prayer of faith would save the sick and that it would forgive sins. It is the joining of these two things which sometimes brings confusion in the matter of healing by prayer. We are certain that forgiveness is in the atonement made by our Lord Jesus Christ when He died on the cross. We are promised that when we believe on the Lord Jesus Christ we shall be saved, that our sins are forgiven. If the promise of healing in answer to prayer is placed on the same foundation as the forgiveness of our sins, we may be led to doubt, for there are times when we pray for healing and are not healed. When someone passes through this experience, he may be led to doubt the fact that his sins are forgiven. At the second coming of our Lord Jesus Christ, the full effects of the atonement will be seen in the redemption of our bodies. In the interim, whether we are healed or not depends upon the will of God.

However, James did connect the confession of one's sins with the effectiveness of prayer. As sins are confessed, they are cleansed by the blood of the Lord. As they are cleansed, an indiviual is justified and as he becomes righteous, his prayer that he may be healed is heard.

James conditioned the efficacy of prayer as coming from an earnest and a righteous individual. The word translated "effectual" in our King James Version, actually means "to exercise strength or power" or "to overcome." The prayer offered in power, or in strength, with ability to bring something to pass, is the earnest or fervent prayer of a righteous man. The word translated "earnest," or "fervent," means "to put forth power," or "to be operative," or "to use energy." It is used to describe the divine power in raising the dead, or in quickening the spiritually impotent. The use of the word itself should rebuke our indifferent, careless, listless prayers. If any man is to receive an answer, he should expect to pray an earnest and fervent prayer. Moreover, James conditions efficacy in prayer to righteousness. This is not righteousness of justification, but it is grounded upon that. Only a justified man is able to be upright before God and to keep the commandments of God. This use of righteousness, however, is the personal righteousness of an individual who walks in accordance with God's law.

The illustration used is of Elijah and his prayer for rain. There was no difference between Elijah and us as to our constitution, our emotions, our weaknesses and our points of strength. Nevertheless, Elijah received an answer to his prayer for when he prayed that it should not rain, it did not rain for three and a half years, and then he prayed again and it did rain. Elijah did his praying and speaking at the commandment of the Lord but he also prayed earnestly, or fervently. One need only turn to I Kings 18:42-46 to get the picture of Elijah's praying fervently. There he shut the world out by putting his face between his knees and seven times prayed unto God, each time sending his servant to the top of Mt. Carmel to look for the signs of rain. Only at the seventh time did he behold a little cloud about the size of a man's hand. James implies that it was a very earnest, profoundly fervent prayer which was prayed by Elijah and which brought forth the rain.

THE PETITION THE WOMAN MADE

This woman had no claim upon Jesus for she was a Canaanite who lived in the area of Sidon. Since she was not of Israel, her faith and her plea were unexpected. She becomes a beautiful illustration of the Lord finding faith in an unsympathetic and incongruous surroundings. In this, the Sidonian woman was much like unto Rahab, the Amorite, who exercised faith in very hostile surroundings.

Jesus had withdrawn from Galilee to the vicinity of Sidon in order to gain rest. He had depleted his energy physically by giving out through teaching, healing and ministering to the multitudes. We ought to learn from Jesus that He intended for his followers to take vacations from time to time. When He saw His disciples tired and worn out, He said, "Come ye yourselves apart into a desert place, and rest a while" (Mark 6:31). Like all those who seek a bit of relaxation and withdrawal, He found that His time was interrupted by the need of a particular person in that area. We find a place of full withdrawal and away from human need is impossible. The woman who stood in need was a remnant of the Canaanites and the Sidonians who were sinners above measure. Their worship of Moloch, Astarte and Baal had degraded them and set them apart as under the condemnation of God. Hence, it was all the more unexpected when this woman came to Jesus asking help. This points up the fact that there are many who live in poverty, in slums, in tenements and even in the midst of vice and crime, and yet who believe in Christ and translate that belief into a beautiful and pure life. The Scripture speaks of saints in Caesar's household. It is possible to be a Christian in the midst of any environment.

This Canaanite woman cried out for mercy and help. Her need lay in the fact that her daughter was "grievously vexed with a devil." This was the woman's own statement and it may have been her interpretation of a situation which was ascribed to a demon and which may only have been a mental and physical sickness. Suffice it to say, her daughter was tormented and in great trouble. There were cases in the New Testament of demon possession, and where the New Testament specifically teaches that a person was demon possessed, we believe that he was. Here Jesus does not refer to the demons, nor does the Bible specifically teach it, so it may have been merely the mother's interpretation of a disease which the daughter had. The mother did identify herself with her daughter.

If we were going to describe the outstanding characteristic of this woman, it is possible that we might say it was her love for her child rather than her faith in Christ. It was love that moved her to come to Jesus; it was love that made her persist in spite of all obstacles. Nevertheless, the Lord Jesus did not commend her love. He commended her faith. Apparently she stood some distance off and cried unto Him, saying, "Have mercy on me, O Lord, thou son of David; my daughter is grievously vexed with a devil." There can be no doubt that she had heard of His healing faculty, of the miracles which had followed His teaching and ministry, of His claims to be the Son of David and the Saviour. Otherwise, she would never have expressed her petition to Him. We are to learn from this that it is wise to express our petitions, to voice them, to make them known. Such expression points out the particular petition which we desire and it also definitely brings it to the attention of the Lord. But to the Canaanite woman's dismay, her petition received no answer. She was merely greeted with the dignity of silence. That silence is a strange thing, for surely it does not harmonize with the deep interest of Christ in the suffering on whom He had compassion. When others had cried unto Him, He had stopped what He was doing, had heard their petition, and had answered it. Perhaps this silence speaks as vocally as any words which our Lord could have said. It is a pregnant silence, full of meaning. Have you ever prayed and found that the heavens were as brass? Have you expected God to speak and found Him continuing in silence?

What was the cause of Jesus' refusal to answer this woman's prayer? There are several explanations of this. One is that the Lord Jesus intended to test the woman's faith, to develop its strength, to perfect her spiritual nature before granting to her this petition. This, however, seems unlike the Lord. Moreover, His later harsh statement would also repudiate it. The second view is that our Lord had to wait until there was a dispensational change before He ministered unto the Gentiles. He declared, "I am not sent but unto the lost sheep of the house of Israel." However, there were other Gentiles to whom He ministered and whose prayers He answered. There is the notable case of the centurion who felt that he was not worthy that Christ should enter under his roof and at whose faith Jesus marveled. There was also the good Samaritan in the parable and the Samaritan leper. But this did not call for the deliberate harshness of saying, "It is not meet to take the children's bread, and to cast it to dogs." It was possible for Him to refuse by silence, but it was not necessary for Him to insult the woman.

Another interpretation is that the Lord here had come to the transition point in His ministry when He was about to announce the imminence of the cross and when He set His face as flint toward the cross. In the next chapter He announced that cross to His disciples and they were unable to understand it. Peter even said, "Be it far from thee." In the statement of Peter he recognized the temptation of Satan and said, "Get thee behind me, Satan." It is possible that in the presence of this Gentile woman he caught a glimpse of the acclaim and faith of the Gentile world and in it He may have recognized the temptation of Satan to abandon the cross. If so, it would explain the harshness of His statement.

Some also think that the Lord here was pointing out to

His disciples and the Israelites that they had had a privileged position, they had seen His miracles, they had received His teaching, they had been the beneficiaries of His ministry, and yet they did not believe. Here was a Canaanite woman who had none of these privileges but who did believe. The Jews called these Gentiles dogs. By this statement Christ pointed out to them that the Gentiles would receive the Gospel when it was taken to them.

There may be some truth in each one of these interpretations. Certainly the Lord declared that He was sent only unto Israel, implying that He had to fulfill the law to die upon the cross, and rise again before the Gospel could be sent unto the nations.

The Persistence of the Woman

Whatever else we may learn from this woman, we may learn the power of persistent prayer. She made four petitions, three of these failed and the final one was answered. Here, then, is emphasized as in so many other teachings of Christ the necessity for persistence in prayer. Each of us may at some time experience this. Our prayer will go up to heaven and we will hear nothing but silence. It is good to remember that the Lord may have other reasons for withholding the answer than merely to strengthen our faith, and it will be well if we resort to persistent prayer in order to overcome these obstacles. Whatever it was that prevented the Lord from answering her petition originally, her persistence and faith overcame it and received a commendation of Christ.

Three qualities stand out: that of worship, humility and faith. This woman had evaluated the person and work of the Lord Jesus and had accepted Him as the Messiah. She gave Him the title of the Messiah; namely, "Lord, thou son of David." She put her trust in Him by saying, "Lord, help me." In this she made the transition from a mere acknowledgment of Jesus as Messiah and the acceptance of Jesus as her Lord.

Her humility was demonstrated in her willingness to consider herself unworthy and as a mere dog in order to get the crumbs from the Master's table. Her quick and witty reply to His statement, "The dogs eat of the crumbs which fall from their masters' table," revealed that she was willing to accept that which was left after the Jews had received His ministrations and benefits. She had been rebuffed by Him, she had been rebuffed by His disciples, and she was willing to take it all and still to persevere. No wonder He held her up as an example unto His disciples of persevering faith which receives an answer.

Her faith rested in His ability, His willingness and His graciousness to answer her plea. Her belief in His mercy made her wishes the measure of His gifts. He said to her, "Be it unto thee even as thou wilt." To us He says, "What will ye that I do?" and then in turn the response will come, "Be it unto thee even as thou wilt." He is able to do exceeding abundantly above all that we ask or think. This woman believed that God was no respecter of persons and that Jesus was the manifestation of God. In this she grasped the Biblical truth that God will hear the prayers of those who come to Him in faith, humility and worship.

This woman's faith was the means of the release of God's power in healing. The Scripture says, "Her daughter was made whole from that very hour." This was the result of her persistence. You may imagine her returning to Sidon, being greeted by a daughter who was well and sound, both of them kneeling to praise God for His wonderful gift and their subsequent life of obedience and faith. All this says that whatever your need, you should lay hold upon the promises of God and say, as did Jacob, "I will not let thee go, except thou bless me."

$\mathcal{D}$orcas

The Woman Full of Good Works

All the widows stood by him weeping, and showing the coats and garments which Dorcas made (Acts 9:39).

Dorcas' life presents a study of a single woman who accepted responsibility in the Christian community until she became a mother to many. Her life was one of kind ministrations to those in need. Her name has since been appended to countless societies of women who are willing to sew for the sake of the poor or who meet together to perform works of love which are inspired by Jesus Christ.

The Hebrew name of this woman was Tabitha which, translated into Greek, is Dorcas, but in English means "gazelle." A gazelle is distinguished for its slender and beautiful form, its graceful movements, and its soft but brilliant eyes. It is like a fawn because of its diminutive size, yet it is graceful, swift, and lovely. In 1932 I was driving a car across the desert of Amman on my way to Petra, when several hundred yards away from the car several gazelles started up. They gracefully ran alongside the automobile but outran it with startling beauty and grace. It is quite possible, therefore, that Dorcas was a beautiful woman, but whether beautiful or not, she was a good woman who was full of good works.

Her name Dorcas implies that she was a Hellenist; that is, a Jewess who lived among the Greeks and spoke the Greek language, but who had become a Christian. We note by the book of Acts that at Pentecost, and again in connection with the testimony and martyrdom of Stephen, there were many Grecians or Hellenists in the Early Church. These also were among the first to go outside Jerusalem preaching the Gospel. It may well be that some of those who were present at Pentecost, or who subsequently heard the Gospel in the various preachings of the apostles and of Stephen, went to Joppa and founded the little Christian church there. As we read of so many Jewish Christians in the New Testament, we wonder why it is so difficult for Jews to become Christians today. Perhaps it is because they feel unwanted in the Christian Church, ill at ease among Gentile Christians, or still the objects of prejudices. Many are the sins committed by Christians in the past of which we Christians today should repent in order that the Jews would feel more at home in our midst. Surely the Church should have many Jews in membership today. We are indebted to them for both the Old and New Testaments, for the Lord Jesus Christ, and for countless spiritual blessings.

The home of Dorcas was Joppa, a name which means beauty. It was a very ancient place said by some to go back to the antediluvian times and to derive its name from Japheth, one of the sons of Noah. However that may be, it is mentioned in the Tel Armana of letters about 1500 B.C. The name means beauty and it is justly applied unto the location of Joppa, which surveys the surrounding countryside and the Mediterranean Sea while being bathed in a mass of sunshine which is reflected from its white, pink, and blue houses. The view from the roofs of Joppa is breathtaking. It was Jerusalem's port, located approximately thirty or thirty-five miles northwest of Jerusalem on the Mediterranean Sea. It was used as the port through which Hiram of Tyre floated the great fir trees of Lebanon in order that they might be taken out of the sea and carried up to Jerusalem for Solomon's temple. Today it is a thriving and well-known port of Israel. In Dorcas' day it was under the jurisdiction of Rome and was a typical port city marked especially by widows who had lost their husbands in the traffic of the sea.

Dorcas had the faith of a Christian. She is referred to as

"a certain disciple named Tabitha." Here is evidence of the spread of Christianity even before the persecution about Stephen. After the preaching of Peter at Pentecost and the conversion of several thousand, among whom were the Grecians, the Gospel was carried by these Grecians to the ports along the Mediterranean. What is described in Acts 11 as occurring in Antioch of Syria undoubtedly also occurred in Joppa. These Christians went everywhere preaching the Word. This is exactly what modern Mohammedans do. They go everywhere preaching their faith and winning converts. Why do not modern Christians engage in the same activity and thus propagate the faith? Dorcas was a Christian. She had heard the Word in the synagogue, her heart had been opened by the Holy Spirit, and her life had been renewed through faith in Jesus Christ. Now she no longer attended the synagogue but was one of the pillars in the church at Joppa. Her faith was exhibited in her works. Paul declares that we are to be careful to maintain good works. James adds that faith without works is dead, and our Lord Jesus Christ declared that a tree is known by its fruits. It is to be expected that a Christian will bear good fruit in the production of good works. Dorcas is described as being "full of good works and alms deeds which she did." The latter describes her treatment of the sick, the poor, the widows, the orphans and the burdened mothers among whom she was an angel of mercy in the community. The former express her works of Christian faith and grace.

The Testimony of Dorcas' Deeds

Dorcas was a woman who dedicated herself to the needs of the many. We have no evidence that she was ever married, although the implication of her name is that she was a beautiful and graceful woman. Therefore, we may assume that she denied herself marriage, family, and home for the sake of the Lord. What a long roster of notable women have done the same thing in the Christian service. One thinks of Jane Adams, of Frances Willard, of Florence Nightingale and of modern missionaries who are attractive girls but who put God's work before their own personal interests and affections. Certainly there will be a compensation from the Lord in the day when we shall all appear before the judgment seat of Christ, that everyone may receive for the things done in his body, according to that he hath done, whether good or bad. The Lord will not be unmindful of our labors of love.

Dorcas did not go to the mission field but she found a field of endeavor at her doorsteps. She was alert to the opportunities which were round about her. Christian women need not regret that they have not had adventuresome opportunities of serving the Lord in notable places. An inventory of opportunities round about their community will present mental hospitals, missions, child evangelism classes, shut-ins, and others who could very well be served. Dorcas did the Lord's work effectively in a quiet and unsung manner. Whatsoever she did she did as unto the Lord (Colossians 3:23).

Dorcas was a woman whose deeds displayed love. This meant entering a home and giving a lift to a distraught family in a time of sickness. One thinks of the mothers who have been overburdened with care and responsibility during time of sickness of their family and have been unable to get any kind of practical help from others. The kind of service Dorcas performed is almost forgotten today. It has come to the point where sickness is prohibitive because of its terrible cost. Dorcas assumed responsibility for some aged people who lived alone and needed the ministry of a friend. Today all too many of them are prey to unscrupulous exploiters. We Christians ought not to relegate such responsibilities to the town nurse, but to assume some of them ourselves. Dorcas accepted the direction and cost of educating some children who otherwise could not be educated. Her work can be duplicated in congregations today where there are women who use their income for the support of those who otherwise would not have opportunity. More women than we know have dedicated their lives to deeds of love as Dorcas did.

The works of Dorcas were recognized in the feeling which the Christian community experienced when Dorcas was gone.

They remembered her self-consuming service, her compassion, her faithfulness, her charity. They knew that they had lost their dearest friend. The picture of these people gathered about in her room weeping does not describe people who are sorry for the things and services they have lost but because they have lost one whom they love.

What Dorcas did for them was what a mother normally does in her family. One thinks of the devotion, the self-sacrifice, the love which is expressed by a Christian mother when one reads in the newspapers of the unnatural brutality, hardness, and neglect experienced and manifested by some women toward their children today.

Dorcas was a woman who mothered the needy, the lonely, the helpless in the church community. The Scripture has a body of teaching concerning the treatment of widows. They were considered to be the responsibility of the church if they had no children, or nephews, to support them, and if they were pious, devout, and prayerful. These the church were to take in charge and to see that they lacked nothing, but if any individual did not care for his own, he was considered worse than an infidel if he allowed the responsibility to fall upon the church. The true widows in Joppa became Dorcas' responsibility and they came to depend upon her. In every Christian group there will be a number of needy persons who will come to depend upon the church and upon its pastor. Think what godly women can do by way of service in such needy cases. They can give themselves to good works in the church by sewing, by nursing, by aiding, and their labors will be recognized of value by God as well as men.

THE TRAGEDY OF DORCAS' DEATH

Because a woman is a faithful minister unto others, is righteous and generous, does not mean that she will be spared the tribulations and trials of life. We may well imagine how Dorcas became tired in her endless errands of mercy and her deeds of kindness. Some of our missionaries who have been on furlough have communicated to me the gruelling demands of their schedules: Rising at five in the morning, treating out-patients by the hundreds during the morning, teaching in the afternoon, performing administrative work following that, doing the rounds again after dinner, and then holding public devotions in the evening until they can do nothing but topple into bed, totally exhausted. How many a mother has found this same experience when the tasks piled up so high that she thought she could never dig herself out and worked long after the rest of the family was in bed. Such tiredness grows from day to day and finally takes its toll.

The time came when Dorcas fell sick. We do not know the nature of her sickness nor the length of it, but it was serious enough to eventuate in death. One wonders how well the others cared for Dorcas during this time, how much she suffered, how many expressions of sympathy and love she received while she was still living. Too often we allow those expressions to go unsaid until it is too late, and then we weep out our love when the individual cannot hear.

In the humble surroundings of her upper room, she found her strength ebbing away. Friends did for her what they could. Finally, when the end was near, the church was called in. Their prayers were ineffectual and the seemingly untimely passing of Dorcas occurred. Many times we refer to the untimely passing of a person because we cannot understand the inter-ruption in their life's activities, yet there is nothing which is not embraced in God's time. Her home-going was a triumph for her as her labors were acknowledged in the presence of the Lord Jesus who must have said to her, "Inasmuch as ye have done it unto the least of these, my brethren, ye have done it unto me." But it was a heartbreak unto others. These widows, orphans, and overloaded mothers felt helpless, much like sheep without a shepherd. No matter what anyone would say or do, they were comfortless, and they continued in their weeping. They performed all the deeds of respect and remem-brance for her which they could, but it brought them no solace. The poignant expression is given describing them showing to Peter the garments and coats which Dorcas had made "while she was with them." Now they knew that she was gone and there was no compensatory help. Many are those who experience similar sorrow and heartache in the loss of their loved ones.

As Christians, they should have known the Christian viewpoint of death, that it is a separation of the spirit from the body, that the spirit departs to be with Christ which, for the believer, is far better, and that the body sleeps until the time of the resurrection. Then a new body, which is incorruptible, immortal, powerful, glorious, and spiritual, is given to the redeemed spirit. A true concept of death does not make for overmuch sorrow except in the sense of loss on the part of those who are left. The Bible leaves no doubt about the fact that to die is to go and be with Christ (II Corinthians 5:1ff; Philippians 1:21; Luke 23:43). The spirits of just men have gone into the presence of Christ to await the advent of the final events (Hebrews 12:22-24; Revelation 6:10).

The Christian message brings the hope of deliverance from death's tragedy through the victory of Christ. Christ tasted death for every man that He might deliver them who all their lifetime were subject to the bondage of the fear of death. His resurrection is the first-fruits of which our resurrection will be the full fruit. The fact that our Lord Jesus arose from the dead should bring comfort to all who pass through bereavement. Therefore the people of God are triumphant over death; they treat it as only a shadow, a transition, a homegoing. His promise is that at death we go to heaven, a better country, a city that hath foundation, a house of many mansions.

The Tribute to Dorcas' God

Upon the death of Dorcas it was learned that Peter was near at hand in the town of Lydda, and Peter was the representative of Jesus whom Dorcas followed. They sent to Peter, requesting "that he would not delay to come to them." Here we have the principle of association. Dorcas was a disciple of Jesus and it was the love of Jesus which manifested itself in her life. They were now in need, so they believed that they could get help through a Jesus man. They knew that Peter was connected with Jesus who could help them. Just as the disciples of John the Baptist at his death went and told Jesus, so these friends of Dorcas, at her death, sought a disciple of Jesus to help them. Their act was one of acknowledgement. They recognized that Dorcas' good works had been inspired by the Lord Jesus who has inspired all such Christian deeds of mercy from that day to this. We should ask ourselves whether the life we live would make men turn to Jesus in the hour of their need. Their act was one of application of faith. They requested Peter to come and help them, to delay not. How similar this was to the request of Mary and Martha who sent to Jesus when Lazarus was ill that he might hasten to their side. Let us not hesitate to call upon Christ or upon His representatives to assist us in the time of need.

After Peter's arrival we have a beautiful picture of a Christian, a man of God who lived in total dependence upon God. Peter immediately wanted privacy. There are times which are too sacred for even sympathetic eyes. He made no promise of what he would do, but he knew where to go. He turned to the Lord Jesus. Peter prayed. We read that he kneeled down and prayed. Here is a reinforcement of the position Christians should take in praying. Probably there came to his mind the case of Elijah's raising the widow's son, of Elisha bringing the son of the Shunammite back to life, of Jesus raising the son of the widow at Nain, and he called these to mind in prayer, claiming the power of God. Probably Peter also appropriated the promises which Jesus had made. And then, with assurance in his heart that God would answer his prayer, he demonstrated the power of faith by turning to the body and saying, "Tabitha, arise." The name of Jesus which had raised the dead, caused the lame to walk, cured the lepers, and given sight unto the blind now caused Tabitha to open her eyes, to see Peter, and to sit up.

The action was a demonstration of the power of God. With quietness but with confidence, Peter invited the widows and members of the church into the chamber and presented her alive to them. Here was a certifying miracle establishing the apostolic authority of Peter and also the truth of the Christian religion. It was only one of several resurrections recorded in the New Testament, but it authenticated the Gospel. Simultaneously, it was an act of mercy on the part of God. The outcome was the establishment of faith and joy in the whole city. God had put his stamp of approval upon the works of Dorcas in caring for the poor, and He had certified the truth of His Gospel. We do not know what became of Dorcas. Probably she lived a long life of usefulness, mercy, and attestation to God's power until she was laid to rest, awaiting the great resurrection of the just.

But it is certain that the immediate cause of the miracle was that "many believed in the Lord." As many had been ministered to by Dorcas in life, so she ministered to many also in this experience. The greatest memory which Joppa has is the memory of Dorcas. How wonderful it is for a godly woman to be the mother of one or of a few, but if she cannot be a mother to one, let her be a mother to many, as was Dorcas.

Lydia

THE WOMAN WITH THE OPEN HEART

And a certain woman named Lydia . . . heard us; whose
heart the Lord opened (Acts 16:14).

The contrast between vision and reality is great. Nowhere
is this brought out more clearly than between Paul's vision of
the man of Macedonia and Paul's first convert in Europe, the
woman Lydia. Great expectations sometimes eventuate in
little experiences.

Paul's Macedonian call is familiar to every Christian (Acts
16:9, 10). A dramatic and moving challenge was given to Paul
and his team in the appearance of the man of Macedonia to
him in a vision saying, "Come over and help us." Innumerable
similar visions have been received by God's people challenging
them to undertake spiritual activity on behalf of needy people.
This has been the motive of many missionary calls. Paul and
Luke, with Timothy and Silas, had intended to go into Bithynia, but were forbidden to do so by the Spirit. Thus, being
deflected from their objective, they waited at Troas for further
guidance. Tradition tells us that Luke was so impressed with
Bithynia that he later made it his home and died there. Bithynia is a place of strikingly beautiful mountains and fertile
valleys. In this interim of waiting, the apostolic party may
have been assailed with doubts as to their guidance. Certainly
they had no intention before this time of entering Europe.
Thus the man of Macedonia was Europe's first great call to the
Christians to come and evangelize them. How strange it is

that Europe is such a great mission field today and the call is being repeated to the Christian Church.

The mission to Europe was immediately undertaken by Paul, Silas, Timothy, and Luke. They made their decision to go into Europe "assuredly gathering that the Lord had called us." One wonders as they crossed the Hellespont, that narrow neck of water connecting the Aegean with the Black Sea and so filled with historic associations, what dreams they had of conquest, of greatness, and of achievement. If their dreams were great, their disillusionment was corresponding when they arrived at Philippi, a Roman colony which out-Romanized the inhabitants of Rome in dress, in manner of life, in class distinctions, in military cliques and in manners. The evangelistic team found that no one was waiting for their help and no synagogue existed where they could even make contact with the Jews. Nevertheless, Luke says, "we were in that city abiding certain days." Where they stayed and what they did, we do not know, but they no doubt surveyed the situation, made inquiries, and attempted to determine where they would first preach the Gospel.

The first meeting attended by and addressed by the apostles was held along the shores of the river which flowed through Philippi into the Aegean. Here was a legal meeting place for Jews and God-fearers, set apart by the authorities of the Roman colony of Philippi. It was not a place of preaching but a place of prayer and worship assigned to the Jews. They apparently had no building but only a grove. It is one more illustration of the fact that believers in God do not need a temple in which to pray. They may meet for prayer in the open places or a barn or a home, as well as in a temple. One almost senses the loneliness of the missionaries as they opened up their work in a new city on a new continent with no friends and no contacts and had only this opening in the place of prayer by the river. They had the additional limitation of being able to speak only to a few women who sat by the riverside making their prayers. We who know St. Paul are sure, however, that in his conversation with these women, Paul made as effective a homily as he ever preached and he was to bear fruit in the conversation of an important woman "whose heart God opened." This was the turning point in the evangelization of a continent. Little do we know whence the fruit of our ministry will come.

THE CASE OF AN OPENED HEART

The woman whose heart God opened was named Lydia and came from Thyatira which was a city in the province of Lydia of Asia Minor. She was a business woman engaged in merchandising dye for which Thyatira was famous. She is described as "a seller of purple." Purple was a name for a dye which was made from shellfish. The fluid from them was first placed on wool, which turned it blue. Then it was exposed to the sunlight, which turned it green, and finally purple. And when it was washed in water it became a brilliant crimson. This was very widely desired and brought a high price. It was used by kings and by the wealthy class. Sometimes decrees were passed by kings that no one in a realm might use this but royalty. Lydia's traffic in purple was either the export-import business, or she was the representative of it in Europe. She represents that large segment of women who have taken an interest in business across the years. Modern women have no monopoly on business acumen. Lydia also is a representative of those professional and businesswomen's groups throughout the world today who are interested in Christian activity.

Lydia was a religious woman, for it is said that she "worshipped God." She was a Gentile but had come to unite herself with the Jews through the steps ordinarily taken by converts to Judaism. First, she had become a hearer of the Word, then a God-fearer, and then finally a proselyte. She was like so many of those noble women in the book of Acts who attached themselves to the synagogues and were worshipers of the true God. They were disgusted and disillusioned with the evils of polytheism and heathenism and had turned to Judaism as the one answer. Lydia gathered regularly with others at the river to worship God and to pray. The most religious people I have ever known have been women, and this religious quality is not incompatible with business acumen and keenness.

Lydia was probably a wealthy woman. This is implied from the nature of her business, from the fact that she possessed a house and had a household. Tradition says that she was a widow with children. How she lost her husband, we have no knowledge, but the fact that she was engaged in this particular business implies that she was wealthy.

Lydia's interest in the Gospel was aroused. "She attended unto the things which were spoken of Paul" (Acts 16:14b). We have sufficient examples of the content of Paul's preaching given to us in the book of Acts to know the things about which he was talking at this place of prayer. We need only refer to Acts 13 and to Paul's sermon in the synagogue at Pisidia in Antioch to know his approach to the Jews. Usually he gave a Scriptural exposition of the history of the Old Testament people, culminating in the coming of, the crucifixion of, and the resurrection of Christ, whom he identified with Jesus of Nazareth. A summary of Paul's message is given to us in I Corinthians 15:1-3 where he makes the death and resurrection the ground of the salvation of one's soul. The intensity, fervency, and charity of Paul in such witnessing is well attested throughout the book of Acts and this would be no exception to his practice. He had no cathedral and no great crowd, but the same intensity and fervency would be manifested in his dealing with these few women. The unction of God was upon him.

As a result, Lydia's heart was convicted. She believed, assented to these truths, and closed with them by faith. Evidently before this time her heart had been closed to Christ even though she was seeking the solace of the true religion. How many times this condition is repeated. Sincere, honest, seeking people, following various religions, sometimes have strong prejudices against Christ and what is actually the truth; but as she listened to Paul, she found her heart opened and drinking in the facts and truths as a thirsty plant drinks in water. There was no more resistance within her. Her heart naturally opened to the truth.

Lydia immediately became a convert of the Christian faith. She believed the truth, committed herself to Christ, and trusted the promise of God for salvation. The change in her came immediately as she listened. How wonderful is a Gospel which will accomplish this. I have often known people to be converted as they sat in their pews listening to the truth as I have expounded the Scripture on Sunday mornings and evenings. Lydia found what she had sought. Her heart was at rest. Her longings were satisfied. She knew the peace of God which passeth all understanding.

The sincerity of Lydia's intention was immediately manifested, because she submitted to the rite of Christian baptism. There is an interval implied between the time of her embracing the truth as presented by Paul in this Jewish place of prayer and her baptism for it was when she was baptized that she appealed to her proof of faithfulness. This could not have happened in a moment's time. It is never wise to baptize a person immediately upon his profession of faith. The missionary practice of making an interval between the two would be wise for the homeland as well. Yet it was inevitable that Lydia should make her confession known. Once she had accepted Christ, she needed to confess Him openly as Lord to be saved (Romans 10:9, 10). By the time that she was baptized, she was judged faithful by the demonstration of her new life.

THE CONDITIONS OF AN OPEN HEART

This story of Lydia reveals to us that there are several conditions which are prerequisites of an opened heart. One is the preaching of the Gospel; another is prevenient grace of God; and another is the personal good will of the recipient.

It is indispensable that the Gospel shall be preached if men's hearts are to be opened for the gift of salvation, for "it pleased God by the foolishness of preaching to save those that believe" and "faith cometh by hearing, and hearing by the Word of God." If hearts are to be opened, it must be because they have heard the Word of truth. It is "by the knowledge of him my righteous servant shall justify many." Thus, we may declare the Gospel to be indispensable. But it must also be intelligible. The presentation of the Gospel must constitute the knowledge of the way of salvation. It must present the fact of the lost state of man, the active and passive obedience of Christ in making an atonement, the necessity of repentance and faith, the gift of the Holy Spirit, and the transformation of human character. Paul was an expert in making this Gospel plain. His presentation of the truth was undeniable. It must either be accepted or rejected, but whether accepted or rejected, it still stood as the truth having been vindicated through the resurrection of the Lord Jesus Christ. Thus, those who heard were left without excuse and facing the imminent judgment, the assurance of which is that God hath raised Jesus Christ from the dead.

The second prerequisite of an opened heart was the prevenient grace of God. There is a divine agency in softening and opening a person's heart. Some hold the view that God regenerates the heart before the exercise of faith on the part of the individual. This is called irresistible grace and is grounded in the elective purposes of God. This theology is debatable and it is rejected by many. It is undebatable, however, that God's grace must attend the preaching of the Word and enable an impotent and spiritually dead sinner to repent and believe. This is called prevenient grace and it goes before any activity on the part of the believer and without it a man cannot be saved. For this reason, all Christians agree that we are saved by God's grace through faith. Lydia's heart was visited by the grace of God so that it was opened to the truth. This is what happens to an individual who upon hearing the presentation of the Gospel finds that without any act of his own will he believes and is ready to respond affirmatively to an invitation to accept Jesus Christ.

The third condition essential to an open heart is the good will of the recipient. This is the activity of the human agency. The fact that Lydia is described as one who worshiped God reveals that she was possessed of a good will, that she sought the face of God. It is necessary for the will of the individual to go into action. This is emphasized again and again in Scripture. We are told that whosoever will call upon the name of the Lord shall be saved, that whosoever will do the will of God shall know, and we are asked, "Why will ye die?" Never is the will of man violated in the matter of salvation. Man is permitted to exercise his moral agency. Holman Hunt's picture of Christ standing at the door and knocking, on which door there is no handle, is accurate. Christ may remove the vines, the hindrances, the bars of prejudice, of ignorance, and of irresolution, but the latch to the door is on the inside. The key to this matter of salvation is the will of man. On the other hand, no man who ever sought the will of God with his whole heart was denied. The promise is that if we will seek we will find, if we will call God will answer; thus, He answered the need of Lydia's heart because she was possessed of a good will.

THE CONSEQUENCES OF AN OPENED HEART

When Lydia's heart was opened, she manifested friendliness to the apostles and also to the Christian message. God opened her heart to the truth and she opened her home to the messengers of the truth. Lydia stands in the New Testament in the position which is occupied by the Shunammite woman in the Old Testament (II Kings 4:10), who prepared a prophet's chamber for Elisha and Gehazi. The principle of hospitality is enunciated in III John 5-8. John was writing to the beloved Gaius, the elder in the church, who had opened his home to the preachers of the Gospel who were strangers to him but not to the Church of Jesus Christ. This action received the commendation of John the beloved and resulted in the praise of Gaius before the church. John declared that this is the duty of Christians and that by the exercise of this duty we are fellow helpers in the dissemination of the truth. No one has kept a prophet's chamber occupied with the messengers of God without receiving a blessing for himself and his family. Often such has resulted in the conversion of the children of the

family or in their call to the mission field or to Christian service
of some other sort. Hospitality to Christian strangers was en-
joined upon the New Testament Church with the reminder
that thereby some have entertained angels unawares (Hebrews
13:2).

Lydia not only offered her hospitality but she pressed it
on the apostles. "She besought us . . . come into my house
and abide." How sincere is your offer of hospitality to Christian people? Do you say, "Sometime come and see me," and
the very indefiniteness of its negates the invitation. Or do you
say, "Wouldn't you like to stay at my home" and the negative
statement of the question implies a negative answer. Not so
with Lydia. She had a sincere, heartfelt desire for the apostles
to come into her home. She actually created a home for these
worthy, weary, worn servants of the Lord who had little in the
form of a home while they were doing the peripatetic work
of the ministry. Lydia was an illustration of the word of Jesus,
"He that receiveth you receiveth me."

Lydia's opened heart developed faithfulness. This is im-
plicitly expressed in the text, "If you have judged me to be
faithful." As we have said, a lapse of time is necessary for the
fulfillment of this text. Faithfulness grows out of faith. In the
Old Testament the word "faith" means *faithfulness*. We cannot
divorce the two. Faith produces works. Lydia wholly identified herself with the apostles and the Christian faith when she
was converted.

Faithfulness is explicitly stated in the reference that the
apostles abode in her home for a considerable length of time.
This is inferred from the description of the bewitched girl's
activities, "this she did many days" (v. 18). As the apostles
went from Lydia's house to the place of prayer and back again,
they were followed by this bewitched girl, calling out that they
were servants of the Most High God. Here we see that there
was no question about Lydia's identification with the apostles
and with the Christians. As soon as she was converted, she
took her stand openly. There is also the tacit expression of
her faithfulness in that she shared the calumny of their perse-

cution. When Paul healed the girl of her spirit of divination, those deprived of their gain seized him, falsely accused him before the magistrates, and beat him. As a result, he was put in prison. The only person available to minister to Paul and Silas in prison was Lydia, and we may well imagine how that she came into this foul place bringing them food and other items of personal comfort. It is only of recent date that prisons have become even remotely respectable. Even as late as one hundred years ago prisoners were manacled, were subject to disease, exposure to cold and sickness and corruption, and were in a despicable plight. Lydia's identification with the disciples certainly must have meant some ostracism for her from the community. This would have an effect upon her business and her social standing, but Lydia was unafraid and was faithful.

Lydia's opened heart resulted in fruitfulness. We read that she was not only baptized, but also her household (v.15). This is one of several household baptisms recorded in the book of Acts (cf. 16:31). Whether these were servants of Lydia or children, we do not know, but the implication is that they were children. Here is household baptism which has to be explained by those who expound the Scripture and hold only to believer's baptism. Moreover, Lydia had a church in her house (v.40). When the disciples were released from prison, they visited with "the brethren" in Lydia's house. This became the meeting place of the church. Thus many churches have begun and thus, also, Christian work should be pursued even in our own day. What a contrast for Paul and Silas between the foul prison and the commodious and comfortable house of Lydia (vs. 35-40). Lydia's opened heart resulted in a true fruitfulness of the Gospel.

Here was the beginning of the church at Philippi and in Europe, a spiritual church which helped Paul in his missionary endeavors and became partakers of his grace. Lydia's stamp was on the church, although in the epistle to the Philippians Paul does not mention her. Here is evidence of what an opened heart can do in the service of Jesus Christ.